Sports Law in Zimbabwe

Sports Law in Zimbabwe

Tinashe Madebwe
Jimcall Pfumorodze
Emma Chitsove
Thabo Fiona Khumalo

This book was originally published as a monograph in the International Encyclopaedia of Laws/Sports Law.

Founding Editor: Roger Blanpain
General Editor: Frank Hendrickx
Volume Editor: Michele Colucci

Wolters Kluwer

Published by:
Kluwer Law International B.V.
PO Box 316
2400 AH Alphen aan den Rijn
The Netherlands
E-mail: lrs-sales@wolterskluwer.com
Website: www.wolterskluwer.com/en/solutions/kluwerlawinternational

Sold and distributed by:
Wolters Kluwer Legal & Regulatory U.S.
7201 McKinney Circle
Frederick, MD 21704
United States of America
E-mail: customer.service@wolterskluwer.com

ISBN 978-94-035-0766-8

e-Book: ISBN 978-94-035-0956-3
web-PDF: ISBN 978-94-035-0966-2

The Authors

Tinashe Madebwe holds an LLB (Honours) and an LLM from Rhodes University in South Africa and a PhD from the University of Strathclyde, United Kingdom. He was previously a senior lecturer in the Department of Law, University of Botswana. He also served as Senior Lecturer at the University of Seychelles, Seychelles. He is currently a Lecturer at Robert Gordon University. He is an avid amateur sportsman and is particularly keen on seeing the growth of sport in Zimbabwe.

Jimcall Pfumorodze holds an LLB (Honours) from the University of Zimbabwe, an LLM (*Cum Laude*) from the University of Western Cape, South Africa and the University of Amsterdam, the Netherlands, and an LLD from the University of Pretoria, South Africa. He is a senior lecturer in the Department of Law, University of Botswana. His research interests are in commercial law and international economic law.

The Authors

Emma Chitsove is a lecturer in the Department of Law, University of Botswana. She specialises in international investment law, law of the World Trade Organisation and environmental law. She teaches Environmental Law, Comparative Legal History and Systems, and Law of Business Associations. Her scholarship concentrates on environmental law, empowerment laws and their implications on Bilateral Investment Treaties, and the regulation of corruption in international investment treaties.

Emma holds a Bachelor of Laws (Hons) from Midlands State University, Zimbabwe, a Master's of Law in International Trade and Investment Law from the University of Pretoria, South Africa, and a Doctor of Laws from the University of Pretoria, South Africa. Prior to joining the University of Botswana in 2016, she was a legal consultant and a practising attorney in Zimbabwe. She was part of the legal team commissioned by the Business Council of Zimbabwe (2011) and the Danish Embassy (2013) to evaluate Zimbabwe's indigenisation and empowerment laws.

Thabo Fiona Khumalo is currently a Lecturer of Law at the University of Botswana. She holds an LLB (Hons) from the University of Zimbabwe and an LLM from the University of South Africa.

Table of Contents

Table of Contents

List of Abbreviations

CAF	Confederation of African Football
CANA	African Swimming Confederation
CEO	Chief Executive Officer
FIFA	Fédération Internationale de Football Association
FINA	International Swimming Federation
FUZ	Footballers Union of Zimbabwe
IAAF	International Association of Athletics Federations
ICC	International Cricket Council
IOC	International Olympic Committee
ITA	Income Tax Act
ITF	International Tennis Federation
NAAZ	National Athletics Association of Zimbabwe
NSSA	National Social Security Authority
NSA	National Sporting Associations
ODI	One Day International
PSL	Zimbabwe Premier Soccer League
SABC	South African Broadcasting Corporation
SRC	Sports and Recreation Commission
UNESCO	United Nations Educational, Scientific and Cultural Organization
WA	World Athletics
WADA	World Anti-Doping Agency
ZAU	Zimbabwe Aquatic Union
ZBC	Zimbabwe Broadcasting Corporation
ZC	Zimbabwe Cricket
ZIFA	Zimbabwe Football Association
ZIMRA	Zimbabwe Revenue Authority
ZOC	Zimbabwe Olympic Committee

List of Abbreviations

General Introduction

Chapter 1. General Background

1. There is a long history of sport in Zimbabwe. This includes all manner of sports from the traditional sports organised by people in their tribes, or, as part of celebrating their cultures, to those sports that came to the country due to colonialism. Football is arguably the most popular one. Regardless, there is a clear appreciation of sport in Zimbabwe. Due to interest in sports and the extent to which investments into sports have been made, it was quite clear that sports needed to be regulated by law and at a central level. Pursuant to this, the Sports and Recreation Commission (SRC) Act was enacted in 1991.[1] It established the SRC which is the supreme sporting body in Zimbabwe tasked with the responsibility of controlling, regulating, assisting, promoting, coordinating and generally overseeing the promotion and development of sport and recreation in the country. The SRC also ensures the proper administration of organisations undertaking the promotion of sport and recreation and promotes the highest standards of sportsmanship and governance.[2]

2. Despite this, there is no dedicated framework of sports law to govern all manner of issues that arise insofar as sport is concerned in Zimbabwe. There also seems to be no will to venture down this path. Instead, the preference has been for sports to be regulated through existing mechanisms. While this has worked thus far, the reality is that, in looking to identify sports law in Zimbabwe, it is essential to parse through several sources of law relevant to sports and, in that way, identify the relevant law pertaining to sports in Zimbabwean law. This is far from ideal. And so the function of this monograph is to compile in one place all the relevant laws that apply to the regulation of all manner of issues that arise in sports law in Zimbabwe. While there is an effort to secure comprehensive coverage, particular attention is drawn to such issues as identifying the sources of sports law, detailing the organisation of sports in the country, with particular attention drawn to such issues as sports governance by the various institutions and a consideration of the public regulation of sport, drawing attention to relevant fundamental rights to the regulation of sport, the restrictions applied when participation is sought, and issues of sports justice. The text also considers employment issues in sports with a focus drawn on such issues as players' rights, their welfare, collective action, and dispute settlement. The text also explores the issue of doping in sport. This is a topical issue on the global

1. SRC Act [Chapter 25:15].
2. *Mukuhlani and Others v. SRC and Others* HH-469-19.

stage and one which the country has looked to tackle head-on. Lastly, the text explores the connection between sport and commerce and identifies how the law looks to govern this relationship while avoiding over-regulation and making recommendations where necessary.

Chapter 2. Sources of Sports Law

3. There is no dedicated body of sports law in Zimbabwe. As such, sport has been regulated using any relevant laws in the country.[3] The sources of sports law in Zimbabwe are, therefore, the general sources of law in the country. Here, it is important to note that, generally, Zimbabwe's law is mainly uncodified and is drawn from several sources.[4] The most prominent and relevant to sports of these sources, which double as the sources of sports law in Zimbabwe, are the constitution, legislation, the common law, and judicial precedent.[5]

§1. The Constitution

4. Zimbabwe is a constitutional democracy. Section 2 of the Constitution of Zimbabwe provides that 'this Constitution is the supreme law of Zimbabwe and any law, practice, custom or conduct inconsistent with it is invalid to the extent of the inconsistency'. And further, 'the obligations imposed by this Constitution are binding on every person, natural or juristic, including the State and all executive, legislative and judicial institutions and agencies of government at every level, and must be fulfilled by them'.[6] This necessarily makes the Constitution the preeminent source of sports law in Zimbabwe. Importantly, the Constitution is a source of sports law in three main ways.

5. First, Chapter 2 of the Constitution, which details national objectives,[7] provides in section 8(1) that these national objectives must guide the state and all institutions and agencies of government at every level in formulating and implementing laws and policy decisions that will lead to the establishment, enhancement and promotion of a sustainable, just, free and democratic society in which people enjoy prosperous, happy and fulfilling lives. Undoubtedly, sport plays a critical role in helping people enjoy prosperous, happy and fulfilling lives. Sometimes this is through actual participation in sport. It is also achieved through owning a club or a

3. Edward Grayson, *Sport and the Law* (2nd ed. 1994). Matthew J. Mitten, et al., *Sports Law and Regulation: Cases, Materials and Problems* (2009).
4. Criminal Law (Codification and Reform) Act [Chapter 9:23] Act 24 of 2004.
5. The constitution entrenches the recognition of African Customary Law in various provisions. In its definition section, law is defined to include any unwritten law in force in Zimbabwe, including customary law. Section 33 instructs the state to take measures to preserve, protect and promote indigenous knowledge systems, including knowledge of the medicinal and other properties of animal and plant life possessed by local communities and people. It further recognises the role of the traditional leaders in resolving disputes among people in their communities in accordance with customary law. Most important is the aspect of establishment of customary law courts whose jurisdiction consists primarily in the application of customary law. Section 176 of the constitution bestows power on Constitutional, Supreme and High Courts to develop customary law taking into account the interests of justice and the provisions of the Constitution. Other Legislation, such as the Customary Marriages Act [Chapter 5:07], Administration of Estates Act [Chapter 6:01], and Customary Law and Local Courts Act [Chapter 7:05] seek to either recognise customary law or provide for its enforcement in certain areas such as inheritance.
6. Section 2(2) of the Zimbabwean Constitution.
7. Section 3(2) of the Zimbabwean Constitution.

team. Other benefits that lead people to enjoy prosperous, happy and fulfilling lives are well established. And so, section 8(1) engenders the state to, *inter alia*, ensure that people can play sport and participate in sport at levels that lead them to live prosperous, happy and fulfilling lives. Separately, section 11 of the Constitution provides that the state must take all practical measures to protect the fundamental rights and freedoms enshrined in the Declaration of Rights contained in Chapter 4 of the Constitution and to promote their full realisation and fulfilment. In addition to this, section 22(1) of the Constitution provides that the state and all institutions and agencies of government at every level must recognise the rights of persons with physical or mental disabilities, in particular their right to be treated with respect and dignity. And, section 22(2) provides that the state and all institutions and agencies of government at every level must, within the limits of the resources available to them, assist persons with physical or mental disabilities to achieve their full potential and to minimise the disadvantages suffered by them. Furthermore, Chapter 2 of the Constitution creates positive and unequivocal obligations on the state to act in the sort of ways that will ensure that all people enjoy their rights and, by so doing, live prosperous, happy and fulfilling lives. Sometimes, this is attained through participation in sports.

6. Section 24 of the Constitution is particularly useful where sport is played at a professional level because it makes provision for work and labour relations. It directs the state and all institutions and agencies of government at every level to adopt reasonable policies and measures to provide everyone with an opportunity to work in a freely chosen activity, in order to secure a decent living for themselves and their families. To this end, the state will endeavour to secure, *inter alia,* the removal of restrictions that unnecessarily inhibit people from working or otherwise engage in gainful economic activities. Subject to the availability of resources, the state also has an obligation to ensure that measures are in place to enable women to enjoy a real opportunity to work. Beyond this, and more directly related to sport, section 32 of the Constitution enjoins the state to take all practical measures to encourage sport and recreational activities, including the provision of sporting and recreational facilities for everyone.[8]

7. Second, Chapter 4 of the Constitution, which is the Declaration of Rights, protects some fundamental rights that are directly relevant to sports in Zimbabwe. For instance, section 48 of the Declaration of Rights protects the right to life, and sport is critical to improving the quality of life of most people, and so participation in sport is an essential aspect of the enjoyment of the right to life. By the same token, section 56 of the Constitution provides for a right to equality which essentially means that no one can be excluded from participation in any sport based on discriminatory considerations. Separately, section 58 of the Constitution provides that 'every person has the right to freedom of assembly and association, and the right not to assemble or associate with others' and that 'no person may be compelled to belong to an association or to attend a meeting or gathering'. This is a critical right with respect to participation in sport because, at its core, sport depends on

8. Section 32 of the Zimbabwean Constitution.

assembly and association. In addition, section 64 of the Constitution is a critical source of sports law because it provides that every person has the right to choose and carry on any profession, trade or occupation, but the practice of a profession, trade or occupation may be regulated by law. Related to this, and particularly relevant to instances where sport is played at a professional level, section 65(1) of the Constitution provides that every person has the right to fair and safe labour practices and standards and to be paid a fair and reasonable wage. And, in terms of section 65(6) of the Constitution, women and men have a right to equal remuneration for similar work. This is reaffirmed in section 80. It provides that every woman has full and equal dignity of the person, and that women should have access to the same political, economic and social opportunities as men.[9] Beyond this, section 68(1) and (2) of the Constitution ensures that there is administrative justice in sport because it provides that every person has a right to administrative conduct that is lawful, prompt, efficient, reasonable, proportionate, impartial and both substantively and procedurally fair and that any person whose right, freedom, interest or legitimate expectation has been adversely affected by administrative conduct has the right to be given promptly and in writing the reasons for the conduct. This essentially means that, at all times, any decision by a public body which adversely affects anyone participating in sport's enjoyment of the sport or of any of their rights can be subjected to judicial review.

8. Third, the Constitution is a critical source of sports law because, to the extent that sport can become an international affair, governed by international codes and prescriptions, section 46(c) of the Constitution empowers courts, when they are interpreting fundamental rights such as those to freedom of association, equality, and fair labour practices, to take into account the international law and all treaties and conventions to which Zimbabwe is a party. In complement to this, section 326 of the Constitution recognises that customary international law, which has periodically dealt with sports law matters, is a part of the law of Zimbabwe to the extent of its consistency with the laws of Zimbabwe. And so, the Constitution establishes international law and custom as sources of law in Zimbabwe to the extent to which this is justifiable.

§2. Legislation

9. Legislation, a reference to written laws with binding effect by an authority entrusted with the power to do so, is a prominent source of law in Zimbabwe. Such

9. Stemming from this provision, the government of Zimbabwe crafted and adopted a National Gender Policy in 2013. One of the objectives of the National Gender Policy is promotion of equal advancement of women and men in all sectors of the Zimbabwean economy and this includes the sports sector.

legislation commonly assumes the form of Acts of Parliament and subsidiary legislation.[10] Importantly for the present purpose, several pieces of legislation, headlined by the Constitution and including Acts of Parliament, and statutory instruments, serve as important sources of sports law in Zimbabwe.

10. To this end, the SRC Act is arguably the most prominent piece of legislation in sports, after the Constitution.[11] This Act constitutes the SRC which is the lead sports regulatory institution in the country. The Act also establishes procedures to be adopted in the registration of National Sporting Associations (NSA).[12] Section 29(4) of this Act grants the Director General the power to cancel or grant a certificate of registration issued to the sports association if the Director General is satisfied that the association does not meet the criteria outlined under subsection 29(4). Section 30 of the Act grants the Minister power upon recommendations from the Board to deregister an association, where an association has failed to comply with recommendations by the Board. In addition, the First Schedule of the Act provides a list of sports that are recognised in Zimbabwe. These sports are not directly regulated by the SRC or the SRC Act, but they have their enabling acts that directly regulate and govern their activities. These different sporting disciplines have different federations which are governing bodies in every sporting discipline that is responsible for the independent administration of each sporting discipline.

11. The sports federations are unions of different sporting associations which are governed by the SRC Act. The purpose of these federations is to bring together the affiliated sports groups and licensed players in different sporting disciplines with the aim of organising competitions. These federations are affiliated with the Ministry of Sports Youth and Culture as well as the Zimbabwe Olympic Committee (ZOC) and they are regulated by the SRC. In addition to all these, the First Schedule of the Act also states that participation in these sports is open to all, including professional athletes and people with disabilities.[13] As a complement to the Act, subsidiary regulations, contained in statutory instruments, have been formulated. For instance, Statutory Instrument 342 of 1995 contains the Sports and Recreation Commission (General) Regulations.

10. In Zimbabwe, the legislative authority of Zimbabwe vests in Parliament, which is the Primary Legislator by virtue of ss 116 and 117 of the constitution. Parliament derives its authority from the people, vested and exercised in accordance with the provisions of the constitution.
11. Chapter 25:15.
12. SRC Act s. 29.
13. Esau Mandipa, *A Critical Analysis of the Legal and Institutional Frameworks for the Realisation of the Rights of Persons with Disabilities in Zimbabwe* (University of Pretoria, South Africa Unpublished master's thesis 2011). It should be pointed that there is a fundamental weakness exhibited by the Act. This is the fact that it uses pejorative language like 'disabled' instead of people with disability. The word is in contravention with the dictates of disability laws and s. 56 which states that: 'every person has the right not to be treated in an unfairly discriminatory manner on such grounds such as their nationality, race, colour, tribe or place of birth, ethnic or social origin, language, class, religious belief, political affiliation, opinion, custom, culture, sex, gender, marital status, age, pregnancy, disability, economic or social status, or whether they are born out of wedlock'.

12. Separately, the fact that employment is a prominent issue in sports means that employment legislation is also a useful source of sports law. To this end, the leading legislation which serves as the primary source of law where employment in sports is concerned is the Labour Act.[14] The Act generally requires employment contracts to be in written form with express terms that establish the nature of the employment relationship. Depending on the nature of the contract, some terms are expected, such as adherence to a code of conduct or determining who will bear medical costs in the case of injury. Employment contracts must also make provisions for remuneration. Another issue that must be addressed in contracts is that of termination of the contract. To this end, section 12(4a) of the Labour Act provides that 'no employer shall terminate a contract of employment on notice unless the termination is in terms of an employment code or, in the absence of an employment code, in terms of the model code made under section 101(9); or the employer and employee mutually agree in writing to the termination of the contract or; the employee was engaged for a period of fixed duration or for the performance of some specific service; or pursuant to retrenchment'. And section 12(3) of the Act provides that 'a contract of employment that does not specify its duration or date of termination, other than a contract for casual work or seasonal work or for the performance of some specific service, shall be deemed to be a contract without limit of time'. There is the proviso that 'a casual worker shall be deemed to have become an employee on a contract of employment without limit of time on the day that his period of engagement with a particular employer exceeds a total of six weeks in any four consecutive months'. Effectively, the Act draws a distinction between casual or seasonal workers, employees on a fixed-term contract, and employees on a limited-term contract. According to section 2 of the Act, casual work is work for which an employee is engaged by an employer for not more than a total of six weeks in any four consecutive months. Importantly, once a contract for casual work exceeds the prescribed period of a total of six weeks in any four consecutive months, it is deemed to have become a contract of employment without a limit of time.[15] Alternatively, seasonal work means work that is, owing to the nature of the industry, performed only at certain times of the year.

13. Separately, section 12(2)(b) notes that fixed-term contracts arise where the employer provides written particulars of the period of time, if limited, for which the employee is engaged. Importantly, in *UZ-UCSF Collaborative Research Programme in Women's Health v. Shamuyarira*,[16] the Supreme Court held that the continued renewal of fixed-term contracts over a period of time does not create a legitimate expectation of re-employment or permanent employment. In addition to

---

14. Chapter 28:01.
15. *Simbi (Steelmakers) (Pvt) Ltd. v. Shamu & Others* ZWSC 71/15.
16. 2010 (1) ZLR 127 (S). This position of the law reaffirmed in *Magodora and Ors v. Care International Zimbabwe* SC 24/14 where the court held an employee on a contract of fixed duration must have had a legitimate expectation of being re-engaged upon its termination and that he or she was supplanted by another person who was engaged in his stead. These requirements are patently conjunctive, and the mere existence of an expectation without the concomitant engagement of another employee does not suffice.

all this, section 17 of the Act empowers the Minister to promulgate regulations covering virtually every aspect of the employment relationship. Regulations made in terms of this section override every contract, agreement, arrangement of any kind whatsoever, determination or regulation made in terms of any enactment which related to the employment of an employee to the extent of any inconsistency.

14. In addition to the above, there is other legislation relevant to sports law which then doubles as a source of sports law. For instance, the Criminal Law (Codification and Reform) Act criminalises a number of acts committed or omitted by people. The other legislation is a source of sports law to the extent that acts may be committed or omitted by people involved in sport. Separately, the fact that significant taxable revenues and incomes are generated through sports means that another important source of sports law in Zimbabwe is the tax law which can be found in tax legislation, with the most notable being the Income Tax Act (ITA).[17] The Act oversees the assessment, payment and collection by the state of tax from individual citizens as well as corporate companies. Another important piece of legislation which serves as a source of sports law is the Finance Act.[18] The Finance Act makes provisions for the revenues and public funds of Zimbabwe, and it works hand in hand with other pieces of legislation related to taxation, such as the Capital Gains Tax Act,[19] the Value Added Tax Act[20] and the ITA.[21] It is also worthwhile to note that the authority to levy and collect tax in Zimbabwe and enforce the provisions of tax statutes has been granted to the Zimbabwe Revenue Authority (ZIMRA) which is a statutory body established by the Revenue Authority Act,[22] making the Act a useful source of sports law. Other important pieces of legislation relate to the protection of intellectual property rights, such as the Copyright Act and Neighbouring Rights Act[23] which contribute to sports law by regulating the protection of the works of sportsmen as well as the logos and trademarks of clubs and associations.

§3. Common Law

15. The common law in Zimbabwe is the Roman-Dutch Law. In terms of section 192 of the Constitution, 'the law to be administered by the courts of Zimbabwe is the law that was in force on the effective date, as subsequently modified'. That law includes the Roman-Dutch Law as applied at the Cape of Good Hope on 10 June 1891.[24] Also, that law was heavily influenced by English Law. Thus, it is best described as Anglo-Roman-Dutch Law. It is also worth noting that the Constitution

17. Chapter 23:06.
18. Finance (No. 2) Act [Chapter 23:04].
19. Chapter 23:01.
20. Chapter 23:12.
21. Chapter 23:06.
22. Chapter 23:16.
23. Chapter 26:05.
24. Section 89 of the Lancaster Constitution which was superseded by the current Constitution provided that 'subject to the provisions of any law for the time being in force in Zimbabwe relating to the application of African customary law, the law to be administered by the Supreme Court, the High

bestows power on Constitutional, Supreme and High Courts to develop common law, taking into account the interests of justice and the constitutional provisions.[25] In its form, the common law consists of unwritten laws that are non-statutory and are not a part of the customary law. And, according to section 3 of the Criminal Law (Codification and Reform) Act, the common law has no applicability to criminal matters. Effectively then, the common law fills the gaps left by the Constitution, legislation, and customary law. Even then, however, 'there is a presumption against alteration in the common law by statute law unless the words of the statute are plain and unambiguous and an intention to later the common law is evident from the wording of the enactment … if the arguments on a question of interpretation are fairly evenly balanced, that interpretation should be adopted which involves the least alteration of the common law'.[26] And, because sports law is regulated by the Constitution and the legislation, the relevance of the common law as a source of law is limited to two main areas.

16. First, recourse to the common law as a source of sports law is in areas where the legislation has not barred the application of the common law. This is most notably the case with respect to the law of contract which is most relevant in employment in sports. While employment is mostly governed by the Labour Act as noted above, aspects of employment remain governed by the common law which generally directs that employment contracts, as with any other contracts, are valid when certain elements are present such as the agreement has to be lawful, with the real possibility of performance, among parties with contractual capacity, holding a real intent to contract, who abide by the formalities that attach to the relevant contracts.[27] Beyond this, the common law also provides that for a contract to materialise, an offer must be made to one person or the public,[28] which is consistent with all the essentials of the contract[29] and an offeree must accept the offer within a prescribed, or reasonable, time[30] and communicate this in clear terms to the offeror.[31] In addition, revocation of an offer is quite acceptable.[32] However, revocation is not effective until the offeree is aware of it. And so, an offer can be revoked at any stage before it is accepted as long as the offeror takes reasonable steps to find and inform the offeree of the revocation.[33]

Court and by any courts in Zimbabwe subordinate to the High Court shall be the law in force in the Colony of the Cape of Good Hope on 10th June, 1891, as modified by subsequent legislation having in Zimbabwe the force of law'.

25. Jimcall Pfumorodze & Emma Chitsove, *The Law in Zimbabwe,* https://www.nyulawglobal.org/globalex/Zimbabwe1.html (accessed 23 Mar. 2020).
26. *Hama v. NRZ* 1996 (1) ZLR 664 (S).
27. *Southampton Assurance Co. of Zimbabwe Ltd. v. Mutuma* 1990 (1) ZLR 12. *Jordan v. Trollip* 1960 (1) PH 825.
28. *Carlill v. Carbolic Smoke Ball Company* 1893 (1) QB 256.
29. *Green Acres Farm (Pvt) Ltd v. Haddon Motors (Pvt)* 1983 (1) ZLR 17 (SC).
30. *Boyd v. Nel* 1922 AD 414.
31. *Levenstein v. Levenstein* 1955 (3) SA 615 (SR). *Bloom v. American Swiss Watch Company* 1914 AD 100.
32. *Bryne and Co v. Lean van Tienhoven and Co* [1880] 5 CPD 344.
33. *Bryne, supra* n. 32, at 344.

17. And so, while the Labour Act may be comprehensive in its coverage of employment matters, any gaps that remain are governed by the common law. For instance, while section 12(4) of the Labour Act governs the time periods that apply when a contract of employment is terminated on notice at the instance of either the employer or employee, the Act does not define the term 'resignation'. Instead, it is left to the courts, using the common law, to establish the actual definition and scope of the term 'resignation'. Importantly, the Supreme Court in *Madondo v. Conquip Zimbabwe (Pvt) Ltd*[34] noted that a resignation is an act of giving up one's job or position on notice or without notice.[35] And so, when gaps manifest, the common law simply kicks in. This is also true with respect to a breach of contract. For instance, in *Guthrie Zhokinyi v. Dynamos*, the Labour Court ruled that despite being banned by Zimbabwe Football Association (ZIFA), Dynamos had not terminated his contract, so it remained in operation.[36] He continued offering his services to the club, but the club just ignored him. Dynamos argued that the ban rendered him incompetent to render any service as to any employer and that there was no reason for formal termination of contract.

18. Second, recourse to the common law as a source of sports law is in areas not really regulated by the Constitution and legislation entirely, such as in delict which engages primarily with 'the circumstances in which one person can claim compensation from another for harm that has been suffered'.[37] For example, in *Edward Sadomba*, the Libyan side Al Ahli Tripoli soccer side acquired Sadomba from Al Ahly Benghazi.[38] The club struck an agreement to pay Sadomba after terminating his contract, but the money was never deposited to him leading the veteran striker to take his case to Fédération Internationale de Football Association (FIFA) and then the Court of Arbitration for Sport (CAS) with the assistance of the Footballers Union of Zimbabwe (FUZ). The court ordered Club Al Ahli to pay Sadomba ZWL 450,000 plus an interest rate of 5% per annum as of 11 January 2016 until the effective date of payment.

19. The law of delict, especially the Acquilian action, is easily applied to people attending sporting events who cause harm. What is a more complicated enquiry is when, and how, to apportion liability when one athlete participating in an event suffers harm due to the actions of another participating athlete. In terms of the law of delict, it would appear that no liability attaches where it can be shown that there is a voluntary assumption of risk. To this end, the common law position derived from several cases[39] is that anyone alleged to have caused harm can rely on the *volenti non fit injuria* defence which holds that a party who voluntarily exercises his/her

34. SC 25/16.
35. Tapiwa G. Kasuso, *Resignation of an Employee under Zimbabwean Labour Law*, 4 Midlands State U. L. Rev. 3 (2017).
36. Staff Reporter, *Dynamos Lose Against Guthrie Zhokinyi*, https://bulawayo24.com/index-id-sports-sc-soccer-byo-104180.html (accessed 14 Jan. 2020).
37. 4 Max Loubser et al., *The Law of Delict in South Africa* (3rd ed. 2018).
38. Petros Kausiyo, *Sadomba Hits Back*, https://www.herald.co.zw/sadomba-hits-back/ (accessed 14 Jan. 2020).
39. Most notably in *Santam Insurance v. Vorster* 1973 (4) SA 764 (A).

will, knowing of the full nature and extent of the risks involved in an enterprise, suffers no injury. Notably, though, there are few Zimbabwean cases on the application of this defence insofar as sport is concerned. The Zimbabwean Supreme Court has noted, however, that the defence is a viable avenue of relief,[40] but this is not available to minors as they do not have the capacity to assume risks so as to be covered by the *volenti non fit injuria* defence.[41] The most relevant consideration when determining whether there is a liability, as per the *Munorwei v. Muza,*[42] seems to be a judicial officer's determination, based on his or her own notions of justice and fair play which are commonly informed by the general norms and sense of values generally prevailing in society, whether liability attaches or not.

§4. Precedent

20. Aside from the above sources of law, Zimbabwean law also places a premium on judicial precedent as a source of law. The doctrine of judicial precedent involves an application of the principle of stare decisis rule, meaning to stand by that which is decided. In practice, this means that inferior courts are bound to apply the legal principles set down by superior courts in earlier cases. In Zimbabwe, Supreme Court decisions are binding on all decisions of inferior courts, thereby ensuring informality and consistency in the application of the law and maintaining certainty and equality of the law in similar circumstances. By the same token, High Court rulings bind the lower courts such as the Magistrates' Courts. This provides consistency and predictability in the law. Here, judicial precedent is a reference to judge-made law in which a previous judicial decision serves as a rule or guide in determining similar cases in the future. Insofar as its status as a source of sports law is concerned, the value of judicial precedent to Zimbabwean sports law is still emerging for three reasons.

21. First, there are not many cases on sports law in Zimbabwe. At best, there are cases that relate to some issues important to sports law, for instance, based on the aforementioned importance of association to sports law, *National Constitutional Assembly v. The President and Others*,[43] wherein Guvava J stated she knew of no right in the (previous) Constitution which forced persons to associate against their will. Indeed, it would be a total negation of that very freedom which section 21 of the (previous) Constitution strives to uphold; particularly, the freedom of association holds some significance. It is clear then that the position in Zimbabwean sports law is that there is freedom of association and the courts will enforce this freedom on account of the legal principles applicable to the need not to interfere with the affairs of Private Voluntary Organisations.

---

40. *See Mutandiro v. Mbulawa* HH-354-84.
41. *S v. Chipinge Rural Council* 1988 (2) ZLR 275 (S).
42. (2015) ZWHHC 804.
43. 2005 (2) ZLR 301 (H) at 316 G.

22. Second, the few sports cases which have been litigated in our superior courts, for instance, the High Court and Supreme Court, rarely result in setting out jurisprudential precedent. The aforesaid observation is borne out from the fact that few sports matters get to be adjudicated upon and determined on the merits in the mentioned courts, thereby depriving various stakeholders in the sporting world, and the judiciary itself, of relevant jurisprudential guidance on a number of sports law issues. The failure to have matters determined on their merits is an issue whose blame may not be imputed to the courts, but an issue which usually emanates from out-of-court settlements between the competing parties.

23. Third, the lack of judicial precedent can also be attributed to the effect of the common refrain that courts of law ought to be slow in intervening in, or interfering with, the affairs of Private Voluntary Organisations.[44] The judiciary's commitment to restraint in this regard has been so extensive that institutions such as Zimbabwe Cricket (ZC) and ZIFA frequently apply their own regulations drawn from parent international institutions, the International Cricket Council (ICC) and FIFA, respectively, as if those regulations are law in Zimbabwe and that they oust the jurisdiction of the courts. Of course, there is prudence in allowing matters to be resolved at the earliest and most appropriate level. However, it is alarming just how much courts have been quite passive here. The most prominent example of an occasion in which the court was when the High Court noted, in *Dynamos Football Club (Pvt) Ltd and Another v. Chiminye and Others*,[45] that it would 'not decline to exercise jurisdiction in football matters on account of FIFA statutes. FIFA statutes do not ouster the inherent jurisdiction of the court. The statutes are binding on its affiliates and not this court'.

44. *See*, Geoffrey Feltoe, *A Guide to Administrative Law and Local Government Law in Zimbabwe* (2012).
45. ZHHC 49/2009.

Part I. Organisation of Sport

24. There are different issues to consider insofar as the organisation of sport is concerned. First, and perhaps at a most basic level, there needs to be a governance framework in place. Once this is done, there is a need to ensure that there is public regulation led by the state. And, lastly, there is a need to make provisions for private regulation. All these important aspects of the organisation of sport are explored in the ensuing sections.

Chapter 1. Sports Governance

25. Governance can broadly be defined as the exercise of power or authority by leadership for the well-being of their constituents or subjects.[46] Generally, effective governance of sports is complex because of the wide range of participants involved. These participants include the leadership; players and clubs; local, national and international organisations; spectators; the media; commercial and non-commercial interests; and educational and training bodies. What particularly complicates governance efforts is that these participants typically have different priorities and interrelationships within and outside the sport.[47] And so, to guarantee good governance in sports, the roles and responsibilities of all these participants should be clearly defined. Good governance also depends on how transparent these roles and responsibilities are defined, monitored and enforced by the governing organisation.[48]

26. Against this backdrop, it is worth noting that sports governance is most prominent at two levels: the international and the national levels. Governance within the state is led by the state and by non-state affiliated institutions. And so, sports governance in Zimbabwe occurs at three levels: the international level where international institutions dictate how sports should be organised, the state level where governmental institutions dictate how sports should be organised, and the state level where non-state affiliated institutions dictate how sports should be organised.

§1. International Institutions

27. Sports governance generally, and in Zimbabwe, is significantly led by the international structures. These structures are typically constituted by states motivated by a shared interest in growing or developing a particular sport, or a particular group of sports, and not for political reasons. Arguably, the most prominent institutions and relevant to Zimbabwe are: International Olympic Committee (IOC); World Athletics (WA); World Anti-Doping Agency (WADA); International Federation of Association Football (FIFA); International Tennis Federation (ITF); ICC; World Rugby and International Swimming Federation (FINA).

I. International Olympic Committee

28. The most prominent institution in international sports governance is the IOC which deals with all Olympic sports, the governance of some of the most popular sporting disciplines in the country such as football, tennis, cricket, rugby, and the

46. Michael Jhon Tamayo, *What Is Governance?*, https://tamayaosbc.wordpress.com/2014/08/21/what-is-governance/ (accessed 25 Mar. 2020).
47. Eddie T.C. Lam, *The Roles of Governance in Sport Organizations*, 2 J. Power, Pol. & Governance 19, 24 (2014).
48. Lam, *supra* n. 47, at 22.

governance of aquatic sports where the country has had notable successes in international competitions. The IOC is a not-for-profit independent international organisation made up of volunteers. The IOC President presides over all its activities, while the IOC Session and Executive Board are responsible for taking the main decisions for the organisation. The IOC generates revenue for the Olympic Movement through several major marketing programmes, including the sale of broadcast rights and The Olympic Partner (TOP) programme. More than 90% of this income is redistributed to the wider sporting movement, which means that every day the IOC provides the equivalent of USD 3.4 million to help athletes and sports organisations at all levels around the world. Quite importantly, for the present purpose, though, over time, the Olympic Charter of the IOC has grown to be recognised as the constitutional charter for the world sports community. The Charter's requirements on governance, which play an important role in sports governance across the world, are that national federations should establish and enforce, in accordance with the Olympic spirit, the rules concerning the practice of their respective sports and ensure their application; ensure the development of their sports throughout the world; contribute to the achievement of the goals set out in the Olympic Charter, in particular by way of the spread of Olympism and Olympic education; express their opinions on the candidatures for organising the Olympic Games, in particular as far as the technical aspects of venues for their respective sports are concerned; establish their criteria of eligibility for the competitions of the Olympic Games in conformity with the Olympic Charter, and to submit these to the IOC for approval; assume the responsibility for the technical control and direction of their sports at the Olympic Games and, if they agree, at the Games held under the patronage of the IOC; provide technical assistance in the practical implementation of the Olympic Solidarity programmes; encourage and support measures relating to the medical care and health of athletes.

II. World Athletics

29. Another relevant institution to sports governance in Zimbabwe, and one which is not quite as big as the ones discussed above but, perhaps equally prominent, is WA. This institution was previously known as the International Association of Athletics Federations (IAAF). Importantly, WA is the international governing body for the sport of athletics, covering track and field, cross-country running, road running, race walking, mountain running and ultrarunning. Included in its charge are the standardisation of rules and regulations for the sports, recognition and management of world records, and the organisation and sanctioning of athletics competitions, including the WA Championships. Beginning in 1982, the IAAF passed several amendments to its rules to allow athletes to receive compensation for participating in international competitions. However, the organisation retained the word amateur in its name until its 2001 congress, at which it changed its name to the IAAF. In June 2019, the IAAF approved a rebranding of the organisation to WA, with a gradual roll-out beginning after the 2019 World Championships in Doha.

III. World Anti-Doping Agency

30. A separate institution, albeit one with ties to the above two institutions, which also happens to be particularly important to sports governance across the world, and in Zimbabwe, is WADA. The Agency was born of efforts by the IOC, in the summer of 1998, to convene a World Conference on Doping, bringing together all parties involved in the fight against doping in sports. This resulted in the First World Conference on Doping in Sport held, in Lausanne, Switzerland, on 2–4 February 1999, which produced the Lausanne Declaration on Doping in Sport. This document provided for the creation of an independent international anti-doping agency, WADA, to promote and coordinate the fight against doping in sports internationally. WADA was set up as a foundation under the initiative of the IOC with the support and participation of intergovernmental organisations, governments, public authorities, and other public and private bodies fighting doping in sports. The Agency consists of equal representatives from the Olympic Movement and public authorities. The main mission of the WADA is the coordination and promotion of an effective fight against doping in sports under the World Anti-Doping Code. Both the thirty-eight-member Foundation Board and the twelve-member Executive Committee of WADA are composed equally of representatives from the Olympic Movement and governments.[49]

IV. International Federation of Association Football

31. Another prominent international institution in sports governance in Zimbabwe is FIFA which is a non-profit organisation that is the highest governing body of football and describes itself as an international governing body of association football, fútsal, beach soccer, and football. FIFA is headquartered in Zürich and has a membership that comprises 211 national associations. Member countries must each also be members of one of the six regional confederations into which the world is divided: Africa, Asia, Europe, North and Central America and the Caribbean, Oceania, and South America. Today, FIFA outlines a number of objectives in the organisational statutes, including growing football internationally, providing efforts to ensure football is accessible to everyone and advocating for integrity and fair play. FIFA is responsible for the organisation and promotion of football's major international tournaments, notably the World Cup which commenced in 1930 and the Women's World Cup which commenced in 1991. Although FIFA does not solely set the rules of football, that being the responsibility of the International Football Association Board of which FIFA is a member, it applies and enforces the rules across all FIFA competitions.

49. Lam, *supra* n. 47, at 23.

V. International Tennis Federation

32. The governance of tennis globally, and in Zimbabwe, is led by the ITF which is the governing body of world tennis, wheelchair tennis, and beach tennis. It was founded in 1913 as the International Lawn Tennis Federation by 12 national associations, and as of 2016 is affiliated with 211 national tennis associations and 6 regional associations. The ITF's governance responsibilities include maintaining and enforcing the rules of tennis, regulating international team competitions, promoting the game, and preserving the sport's integrity via anti-doping and anti-corruption programmes. The ITF partners with the Women's Tennis Association (WTA) and the Association of Tennis Professionals (ATP) to govern professional tennis. The ITF organises the Grand Slam events, annual team competitions for men (Davis Cup), women (Fed Cup), and mixed teams (Hopman Cup), as well as tennis and wheelchair tennis events at the Summer Olympic and Paralympic Games on behalf of the IOC. All these events are quite popular in Zimbabwe with the Davis Cup, in particular, having captivated the interest of the country in the past.

VI. International Cricket Council

33. Because cricket is a quite popular sport in Zimbabwe, it is useful to note that the governance efforts of the ICC are a particularly important part of the sports governance landscape of the country. Thus, there is value in noting that the Council is the global governing body of cricket. It was founded as the Imperial Cricket Conference in 1909 by representatives from Australia, England and South Africa. It was renamed the International Cricket Conference in 1965 and took up its current name in 1989. The ICC has 104 members and Zimbabwe is one of the twelve full members that play Test matches. Of note, the ICC is responsible for the organisation and governance of cricket's major international tournaments, most notably the Cricket World Cup. It also appoints the umpires and referees that officiate at all sanctioned Test matches, One Day International (ODI) and Twenty20 Internationals. It promulgates the ICC Code of Conduct, which sets professional standards of discipline for international cricket, and also coordinates action against corruption and match-fixing through its Anti-Corruption and Security Unit (ACSU). Further, the ICC does not control bilateral fixtures between member countries (which include all Test matches), and, importantly, it does not govern domestic cricket in member countries, and it does not make the laws of the game, which remain under the control of the Marylebone Cricket Club. Despite this, the Council wields extensive power as it can suspend membership any time its rules, particularly those related to no political interference in the sport, are violated. Such suspensions have such extensive financial implications for suspended states that every effort is made in sports governance in these states to ensure the rules are not violated. This is particularly important in the Zimbabwean context because, quite recently, the ICC suspended

Zimbabwe from international competition for government interference.[50] This followed the unanimous decision by the ICC Board that ZC, an ICC Full Member, was in breach of the ICC Constitution which imposes an obligation on members to provide a process for free and democratic elections and to ensure that there is no government interference in its governance and/or administration for cricket respectively.

VII. World Rugby

34. Rugby's status as a popular sport in Zimbabwe has also meant that the international governance of rugby is important in Zimbabwe. Such governance efforts are led by World Rugby, the world governing body for the sport of the Rugby Union. It was founded as the International Rugby Football Board (IRFB) in 1886 by Scotland, Wales and Ireland, with England joining in 1890. Australia, New Zealand and South Africa became full members in 1949. France became a member in 1978 and further eighty members joined from 1987 to 1999. The body was renamed the International Rugby Board (IRB) in 1998 and took up its current name of World Rugby in November 2014. World Rugby organises the Rugby World Cup every four years, the sport's most recognised and most profitable competition. It also organises a number of other international rugby competitions, such as the World Rugby Sevens Series, the Rugby World Cup Sevens, the World Under 20 Championship, and the Pacific Nations Cup. Zimbabwe has participated in some of these competitions.

VIII. International Swimming Federation

35. The last governance institution worth taking note of here, rooted in the fact that aquatic sports are popular in Zimbabwe, and the fact that Zimbabwean athletes have had some notable successes in these sports on the international stage, is the FINA which is the international federation recognised by the IOC for administering international competition in water sports. It is one of several international federations which administers a given sport or discipline for the IOC and the international community. FINA currently oversees competition in six aquatics sports: swimming, diving, high diving, artistic swimming, water polo, and open water swimming. FINA also oversees 'Masters' competition (for adults) in its disciplines. And so, all manner of aquatic competitions should be sanctioned by FINA and align with the institution's rules.

---

50. BBC Sport, *ICC Suspends Zimbabwe Cricket for Political Interference*, https://www.bbc.com/sport/cricket/49038834 (accessed 20 Jul. 2019).

§2. Governmental Institutions and Bodies

36. Zimbabweans' love of sport and the fact that several issues of public concern attached to the sport, such as revenue generation, employment, gambling, cheating in sport, have always meant that there was a need for the state to put in place an institutional governance framework. Such framework is tailored towards ensuring that there is sports governance that leads to satisfactory results for all parties concerned whether they are directly involved in sport or just concerned about the governance in sport generally.

37. The most prominent, and overarching, state institution in Zimbabwean sports law charged with sports governance is the Ministry for Sport, Arts and Recreation. Of note, the Ministry has created a Portfolio Committee on Youth, Sports and Recreation which is charged with examining the expenditure, administration and policy of the Ministry and other matters falling under their jurisdictions as Parliament may by resolution determine.[51] At the head of the Ministry is the Minister of Sport, Arts and Recreation. Under the Minister is the Permanent Secretary. For the most part, however, most sports governance activities are carried out by the Director of Sport who is tasked with administering all sports policies and activities and reporting directly to the Minister. In the performance of his mandate, the Director will be assisted by another government institution which is quite prominent in sports governance in Zimbabwe, the SRC. The Commission is led in this effort by the SRC Board,[52] whose powers include managing, controlling and administering the assets of the SRC. One of the more notable functions of the Board of the SRC is the task of appointing a Director General who is to hold office for a term of three years, renewable only once. The Director is under the general direction and control of the Board and is responsible for the day-to-day operations and administration of the SRC.

38. The SRC Act which creates the Commission also establishes the SRC Fund which is a fund to which all proceeds of any lottery and investments shall be an aid and out of which financial support for sportspersons and sports organisations shall be paid out. The Fund is managed, controlled and administered by a Board of Trustees, which is a body corporate with perpetual succession. Other functions of the Board include managing, controlling and administering the assets of the Fund. The Chief Executive Officer (CEO) of the Board of Trustees to the Fund is responsible for the management of the affairs and the transactions of the Board of Trustees and the exercise, discharge and performance of the objectives, functions and duties of the Board of Trustees.

---

51. Zimbabwe Government, *Introduction to Committees in Parliament*, https://www.parlzim.gov.zw/about-parliament/committee-system (accessed 23 May 2019).
52. SRC Act s. 3.

39. The Commission has the power to suspend any sports governing authority's functions. For instance, in June 2019, the SRC suspended the entire ZC Board alleging corruption and election irregularities.[53] Quite related, sports governance in terms of the SRC Act also relies on the work of the Directorate of Sports and Youth Affairs. This Directorate is charged with the promotion of sports and games and youth welfare programmes. It also works with the SRC to monitor the functioning of the provincial sports offices, state, district and sports associations, and clubs and schools undertaking sports activities in the country.

40. Importantly, the role of all the institutions created by the SRC was enhanced when section 32 of the Constitution imposed an obligation on the state to take all practical measures to encourage the sport and recreational activities, including the provision of sporting and recreational facilities for everyone. It will be interesting to see how other institutions created by the Constitution will evolve to facilitate this. Already, there is an Anti-Corruption Commission,[54] and this is a potentially important institution in encouraging sports and recreational activities, including the provision of sporting and recreational facilities for everyone on a corruption-free basis. By the same token, the fact that enjoyment of, and participation in, sport hinges on the availability of several rights, it becomes clear that the Zimbabwe Human Rights Commission is a potentially important institution in encouraging sport and recreational activities, including the provision of sporting and recreational facilities for everyone.[55]

§3. Non-governmental Institutions

41. Aside from the international and national level state-controlled sports governance institutions, Zimbabwean sports law also features several institutions which are critical to sports governance but are non-governmental in nature. Consistent with the approach above, the discussion will draw focus on the governance efforts by the ZOC which deals with all Olympic sports, and those institutions involved in the governance of some of the most popular sporting disciplines in the country, or disciplines in which the country has had notable successes in international competitions, such as football, tennis, cricket, rugby, and aquatic sports.

42. The ZOC is probably the most prominent non-governmental institution involved in sports governance in Zimbabwe. Of note, the ZOC was created in 1934 and recognised by the IOC in 1980. The Committee has a Constitution and is governed by the General Assembly which meets annually. In between General Assemblies, the Executive Board takes charge of ZOC business. The Board is elected every four years in the year following the Olympic Games. In addition to this, the

53. Law in Sport, *INTERPOL Integrity in Sport Bi-Weekly Bulletin – 30 July 2019–12 August 2019,* https://www.lawinsport.com/topics/item/interpol-integrity-in-sport-bi-weekly-bulletin-30-july-2019-12-august-2019 (accessed 1 Aug. 2019).
54. Sections 254–257 of the constitution.
55. Sections 242–243 of the constitution.

ZOC also has a Secretariat of six full-time staff members headed by the CEO/ Secretary General, but, like many other sporting organisations in Zimbabwe, benefits considerably from the involvement of volunteers. Its objective is to develop and protect the Olympic Movement in Zimbabwe in accordance with the Olympic Charter. Presently, the ZOC has thirty National Sports Associations affiliated with it on a voluntary basis. It is also worth noting that sporting associations that are created and registered with the SRC in terms of the SRC Act can also affiliate with the ZOC. Importantly, the ZOC is heavily involved in efforts to enhance sports governance. In September 2019, for instance, the Committee organised a governance strategy and policy development workshop for national federations to help them promote and develop sustainable sport.[56] Of note, the ZOC works closely with the National Athletics Association of Zimbabwe (NAAZ), which is the body charged with regulating athletics in Zimbabwe.

43. Another well-established non-governmental institution that contributes to the governance of sport in Zimbabwe is the ZIFA. This is the governing body of football in Zimbabwe. It is responsible for organising the national football competitions in Zimbabwe and the Zimbabwe national football teams. The current ZIFA was founded in 1979. It has been affiliated with FIFA since 1965 and has been a member of the Confederation of African Football (CAF) since 1980.

44. Zimbabwe Premier Soccer League (PSL) is the top professional division of the ZIFA. It was created in 1980, as a successor to the 1962-formed Rhodesia National Football League. It is currently sponsored by Delta Beverages under the Castle Lager brand and hence is known as Castle Lager PSL. The current sponsorship deal runs from 2021 and is worth USD 3.6 million. The league has traditionally been made up of that play a total of thirty-four matches each. The season runs from April to November. Most matches are played during weekends on Saturdays and Sundays. Postponed matches are played midweek. The end-of-season winner qualifies for the CAF Champions League, while the Cup of Zimbabwe winners gain entry into the CAF Confederation Cup. On hand, four teams are relegated to the lower division and an equal number are promoted. Most importantly, for governance purposes, perhaps, the League has a set of rules that are probably the most comprehensive in Zimbabwean professional sports. As such, they are quite useful generally.

45. In addition to the above institutions, as cricket is the most popular sport in Zimbabwe after football, its governance is of particular interest. To this end, it is worth noting that the governance of cricket in Zimbabwe is presided over by ZC (formerly known as the ZC Union). Of note, ZC is a full member of the ICC and African Cricket Association. It operates the Zimbabwean cricket team and organises Test tours, ODIs with other nations and domestic cricket in Zimbabwe. Thc

56. Nancy Gillen, *Zimbabwe Olympic Committee Run Governance Strategy Workshops for National Sport Associations*, https://www.insidethegames.biz/articles/1084524/zimbabwe-olympic-committee-governance (accessed 20 Mar. 2020).

national team has had successes in the past with Andy Flower, a Zimbabwean batsman, who was once considered as one of the top-ranked batsmen in the world.[57] In recent years, however, performances have been poor, and this has been attributed to several factors, including the governance of the sport, which has been accused of being politically compromised. Most recently, as noted above, the ICC suspended Zimbabwe from international competition for government interference. This followed the unanimous decision by the ICC Board that ZC, an ICC Full Member, was in breach of the ICC Constitution which imposes an obligation on members to provide a process for free and democratic elections and to ensure that there is no government interference in its governance and/or administration for cricket respectively.

46. Quite separately, the fact that rugby is another sport that Zimbabweans appreciate, and that national teams have had some successes on the international stage, makes the governance of the sport of interest here. To this end, it is worth noting that all aspects of rugby in Zimbabwe are governed by the Rugby Union. Despite all these efforts, the country's lack of infrastructure and largely rural population has been a problem for national organisers. Consequently, unlike other neighbouring African countries, Zimbabwean rugby has been dominated, first, by a white settler class and second, by the wealthy. In reality, then, rugby has not achieved the kind of integration that it should have. Attempts to increase participation among the black and poor population groups have occupied governance efforts. However, these have yielded mixed results. And so, present governance efforts are quite preoccupied with finding effective ways in which to address these issues.

47. Yet another important institution in sports governance in Zimbabwe, rooted in the country's long-standing successes in water sports, is the Zimbabwe Aquatic Union (ZAU). The Union was established in terms of Article 1 of the Zimbabwe Aquatic Constitution[58] and is an affiliate of the African Swimming Confederation (CANA), which is the governing body for each aquatic discipline within Africa. The Union is also an affiliate of the FINA, which is the IOC recognised world governing body in international competitions in aquatic disciplines such as swimming, diving, water polo, open water swimming, synchronised swimming and masters swimming. In terms of Article III[59] of the ZAU Constitution, the Union has jurisdiction over all matters pertaining to aquatic disciplines within Zimbabwe.

---

57. ICC, *25 Years of Zimbabwe in Test Cricket*, https://www.icc-cricket.com/news/498590 (accessed 30 Jul. 2019).
58. Article 1 of the Zimbabwe Aquatic Union Constitution and Bye Laws of 2009 provides that 'The Federation shall be called the Zimbabwe Aquatic Union Constitution and Bye Laws (2009) … which shall be affiliated to FINA (Fédération International de Natation Amateur) and CANA (Confédération Africaine de Natation Amateur).'
59. *See* Zimbabwe Aquatic Union Constitution and Bye Laws (2009).

Chapter 2. Public Regulation

48. The public regulation of sports is a particularly important issue because sports and the practices or decisions made by participants as well as those involved in sports in any way are very often a national concern for several reasons. For instance, mere participation in sports is a crucial issue, especially with the directive in section 32 of the Constitution, that the state should take all practical measures to encourage sports and recreational activities, including the provision of sporting and recreational facilities for everyone. Separately, public regulation is also important because several rights and civil and criminal liabilities attach to participation in sport, and so, it becomes essential to ensure that all this is sufficiently regulated. In addition, sports generate revenue, and such issues as how this revenue is shared, whether participants get fair remuneration, as well as the control of this revenue, and whether the revenue is taxed, are very often matters of public concern. The same is true in those instances where disputes arise. The fact that so many people are invested in sports means that sports justice is a quite prominent issue that must be the focus of public regulation efforts.

§1. Fundamental Rights

49. Chapter 4 of the Constitution, the Declaration of Rights, makes provision for several fundamental rights and freedoms which are instrumental to the public regulation of sports. Most important among these rights is section 58 of the Constitution which provides that, 'every person has the right to freedom of assembly and association, and the right not to assemble or associate with others' and that 'no person may be compelled to belong to an association or to attend a meeting or gathering'. This is a particularly important right insofar as sport is concerned, where an individual can enjoy the sport more effectively in cooperation with others because it effectively protects contact with others and cooperation for joint purposes. An individual is, therefore, free to form and join associations and participate in their activities and pursue goals freely.

50. It is also worth noting that association and participation in sports generally should not be limited by discriminatory practices. To this end, section 56 of the Constitution provides that everyone should be treated equally regardless of their nationality, race, colour, tribe, place of birth, ethnic or social origin, language, class, religious belief, political affiliation, opinion, custom, culture, sex, gender, marital status, age, pregnancy, disability or economic or social status, or whether they were born in or out of wedlock. And so, there can be no discrimination of any kind in the organisation of sport. In order to be acceptable, discrimination would have to be fair, reasonable and justifiable in a democratic society based on openness, justice, human dignity, equality and freedom.[60] Discrimination is acceptable if it takes into account

60. Pfumorodze & Chitsove, *supra* n. 25.

all relevant factors, including the nature of the right or freedom concerned; the purpose of the limitation, in particular, whether it is necessary in the interests of defence, public safety, public order, public morality, public health, regional or town planning or the general public interest; the nature and extent of the limitation; the need to ensure that the enjoyment of rights and freedoms by any person does not prejudice the rights and freedoms of others; the relationship between the limitation and its purpose, in particular, whether it imposes greater restrictions on the right or freedom concerned than are necessary to achieve its purpose; and whether there are any less restrictive means of achieving the purpose of the limitation.[61]

51. In addition to these rights, the Constitution looks to protect rights of publicity or personality rights, which grant an individual the right to control the commercial use of his or her identity, such as name, image, likeness, or other unequivocal identifiers. These rights are important in sports as they allow athletes to benefit from the sale and distribution of products featuring their likeness, for instance. In practice, few countries have recognised this right, and Zimbabwe is no exception. However, the Constitution does protect these rights through the provision in section 57 that provides that every person has the right to privacy. In complement to this, section 71(2) of the Constitution protects every person's right, in any part of Zimbabwe, to acquire, hold, occupy, use, transfer, hypothecate, lease or dispose of all forms of property, either individually or in association with others.

§2. Governmental Conditions and Permits

52. One of the most important consequences of sport being such a universally appreciated activity and one which appeals to several people of different nationalities, coupled with the fact that significant revenues can be generated from sport, is that government regulation of participation in sport by different people becomes a key issue. In particular, governmental interventions are necessary when the issue of foreigners' participating in sports arises. Related to this and in light of section 20 of the Constitution,[62] governmental interventions are also important to establish quotas and conditions for participation that will ensure that constitutional directives are met.

53. Now, with respect to the issue of foreigners' participation in sport, it is essential to note that the general position, drawn from section 32 of the Constitution which provides that the state should take all practical measures to encourage sports and recreational activities, including the provision of sporting and recreational facilities for everyone, is that all persons in Zimbabwe can participate in sport.

61. Section 86(2) of the constitution.
62. Section 20 of the constitution calls on the state and all institutions and agencies of government at every level to take reasonable measures, including affirmative action programmes, to ensure that youths, between the ages of 15 and 35 years, have access to appropriate education, training; are afforded opportunities for employment and other avenues to economic empowerment; and have opportunities for recreational activities and access to recreational facilities.

Notably, though, the need to accommodate and protect the greater public interest means that three main circumstances will often arise where conditions may be applied to such participation.

54. The first circumstance where conditions on participation may be imposed, rooted in the need to secure distributive justice, is when quotas on participation are imposed. In a strict sense, quotas may appear to go against meritocracy and equality. However, it is vital to note that equality is distinguished from similarity, and so, there will be instances where attaining equality will require treatment that is dissimilar. It is the justifiable pursuit of equality in this form which serves as the rationale that informs the turn to quotas in sports regulation. On the same note, it is worth noting that quotas are also consistent with section 10 of the Constitution which provides that the state and every person, including juristic persons, and every institution and agency of government at every level, must promote national unity, peace and stability. Experience across the world suggests that an institutionalised approach to empowerment which, in sport at least, sometimes assumes the form of quota setting is critical to the promotion of national unity, peace and stability. Further, the justification for the turn to quotas in modern Zimbabwe is section 14 of the Constitution, which provides that the state and all institutions and agencies of government at every level must endeavour to facilitate and take measures to empower, through appropriate, transparent, fair and just affirmative action, all marginalised persons, groups and communities in Zimbabwe. In addition, section 18 of the Constitution directs the state to ensure that 'all institutions and agencies of the State and government at every level must take practical measures to ensure that all local communities have equitable access to resources to promote their development'. Some such resources can be generated through participation in sports. And so, the state may have to ensure that underrepresented regions and people are represented in sports or are assisted to secure such representation and participation.

55. In the same vein, the turn to quotas is justifiable in terms of section 22(1) of the Constitution which provides that the state and all institutions and agencies of government at every level must adopt reasonable policies and measures, within the limits of the resources available to them, to provide everyone with an opportunity to work in a freely chosen activity, in order to secure a decent living for themselves and their families and, section 22(2) which provides, *inter alia*, that the state and all institutions and agencies of government at every level must endeavour to secure full employment and the removal of restrictions that unnecessarily inhibit or prevent people from working and otherwise engaging in gainful economic activities. It is worth noting that, in sports participation at least, the government seldom establishes quotas at the central level. Different sports agencies are allowed to address quota issues in ways appropriate to the discipline in question. For instance, the PSL Rules and Regulations provide that no soccer club may sign or register more than five foreign players during the course of any particular season, even if previously registered foreign players are deregistered during the course of the season.[63] A club may only field three foreigners in any competitive matches organised by PSL and

63. Order 4.3 of Premier Soccer League (PSL) Rules and Regulations 2015 as amended.

ZIFA. Importantly, the PSL Rules and Regulations provide that a foreign player is ineligible to represent Zimbabwe in terms of the statutes of FIFA.[64] Notwithstanding this, in terms of the PSL Rules and Regulations, a foreign player who has obtained permanent residence in terms of the Immigration Act, or similar legislation, or a foreign player who has been granted refugee status in accordance with the applicable laws of the Republic of Zimbabwe, shall not be regarded as a foreign player for the purpose of the regulations.[65]

56. Separately, the second circumstance where conditions on participation may be imposed, rooted in the need to drive the sports agenda forward, has resulted in the adoption, for the sake of fair play and equity, of several conditions for participation in sports that are intended to ensure that there is no discrimination and that there is responsible growth of sport. A most notable example relates to the requirement that coaches of professional sporting teams should hold basic minimum qualifications. And so, law and treatment under law will amount to discrimination if it prejudices persons by imposing restrictions or disabilities on persons or by withholding privileges or advantages wholly or mainly on the basis of their political opinions, sex, race, ethnicity or religion.

57. The third circumstance where conditions on participation may be imposed, also rooted in the desire to advance the growth of Zimbabwean sport, is when conditions are imposed on the participation of foreigners in local sports. The general position is that all foreigners can participate in any sport when their immigration status allows. And the country has always encouraged skilled foreign nationals to come and impart knowledge to locals, particularly in educational institutions. The ability of foreign nationals to represent the state in international events is governed by the international organisation which regulates the state. These organisations generally leave it to the state to determine the level of affiliation necessary for the person to represent the state.[66] Where they should be employed in the sports sector, they can only do so with a work permit. To this end, section 41 of the Constitution enjoins Parliament to establish the Citizenship and Immigration Board responsible for: granting and revoking citizenship by registration; permitting persons, other than citizens, to reside and work in Zimbabwe and fixing the terms and conditions under which they may so reside and work; and exercising by any other functions that may be conferred or imposed on the Board by or under an Act of Parliament. Persons wanting to come to Zimbabwe for purposes of employment are normally allowed entry only if the prospective employers can show to the satisfaction of the Foreign Recruitment Committee that the required skills are not available locally and that they have been unable to recruit from within the country. The prospective immigrant is then granted a residence permit and temporary employment permit allowing them to work only for that particular organisation and for a limited period of time (usually two to three years in the first instance). The temporary employment

64. Order 4.1 of Premier Soccer League (PSL) Rules and Regulations 2015 as amended.
65. Order 4.2 of the Premier Soccer League (PSL) Rules and Regulations 2015 as amended.
66. FIFA has stricter regulations on who may represent a state and the number of foreign nationals who may represent the state.

permit will normally not be granted for a period exceeding five years, including any periods of renewal.[67] The holder of a temporary employment permit is not allowed to change occupations or employers during the period specified in the permit.[68] In the meantime, the employing organisation is expected to put in place a training programme for a Zimbabwean resident to understudy the expatriate worker.

§3. Criminal and Civil Liability

58. The high number of participants in sports, which include the leadership, players and clubs, local, national and international organisations, spectators, the media, commercial and non-commercial interests, and educational and training bodies, means that conflicts are inevitable. In Zimbabwean law, these conflicts assume a criminal or civil quality which determines whether there is civil or criminal liability. To explain further, criminal liability, where it arises, is regulated based on the Criminal Law (Codification and Reform) Act. The Act criminalises several acts and establishes when a person will be liable. The burden of proof in these instances is 'proof beyond a reasonable doubt'. It is also worth noting that establishing criminal liability is also often dependent on an actor having a culpable state of mind but is not necessarily so in respect of conduct where an act is prohibited regardless of the state of mind of the offender. The situation is different with respect to civil liability which most commonly arises where disputes between citizens or between citizens and the state arise. These disputes are often rooted in delict, contract, labour law, and commercial transactions.[69] Importantly, to establish civil liability, one has to show that the offending party intended to cause harm or negligently caused the harm, knowing fully that harm could result. Because people have such an interest in sports, it is inevitable that conflicts leading to criminal and civil liability will arise and the resolution of these is a public interest and so, a public regulation concern. And, it would appear that the central approach to criminal and civil liability issues has resulted in established law on the approach to liability as it relates to four categories of participants.

I. Athletes and Personnel Involved in an Event

59. It is important to begin by noting here that athletes across the world were traditionally not empowered to sue for actions of other athletes during games, bouts, or matches. Drawing from jurisdictions applying the same law as Zimbabwe, however, this position changed over time as the approach to negligence and liability evolved, and it has been accepted that the test for establishing liability is whether a duty of care was owed to the claimant or victim as a person reasonably foreseen to be affected by the act of the offender; the duty so established must be breached by

67. Section 22 of the Immigration Regulations, 1998 – as amended by SI. 126/05.
68. Section 23 of the Immigration Regulations, 1998 – as amended by SI. 126/05.
69. *See*, Geoffrey Feltoe, *A Guide to the Zimbabwean Law of Delict* (2013). *Also see*, Alistair J. Kerr, *Principles of the Law of Contract* (4th ed. 1989).

the offender and whether the claimant or victim suffered some injury or damage due to the breach.[70] And, in the modern world, following the seminal *Condon v. Basi*,[71] where the plaintiff's leg was broken as the result of a 'foul' sliding tackle by the defendant during a local league match, the decision by the English Court of Appeal that a sports participant owes a duty of care to an opponent to take reasonable care in all circumstances is now widely accepted as reflecting the standing position on the civil and criminal liability of athletes and personnel involved in an event. Effectively then, a duty of care is therefore owed by athletes to fellow athletes,[72] coaches, governing bodies and sports officials. And so, an athlete may be guilty of committing an intentional delict along with a criminal act of assault and battery for any actions taken during a game, match, or event.[73] Certain sportsmen, such as boxers, could also find themselves on the wrong end of the public laws, should they cause the death of their opponents in the course of engaging in a boxing contest, regardless of whether or not they had intentions of so doing.

60. Despite all this, it remains the case that negligence is hard to prove in sports, where, depending on the sport, violent actions and injuries are more common and thus more expected. This has two implications for liability. 'First, the threshold of liability is in practice inevitably high. The breach of a duty will not flow from proof of no more than an error of judgment or momentary lapse in skill when subject to the stresses of a race. In practice it may be difficult to prove any such breach of duty absent proof or conduct that in point of fact amounts to reckless disregard for the fellow contestant's safety.'[74]

61. Second, and related to an issue discussed previously, it means that participants are considered to have assumed the risk of injury. Here, the Zimbabwean common law position is that anyone alleged to have caused harm can rely on the *volenti non fit injuria* defence which holds that a party who is not a minor but voluntarily exercises his/her will, knowing of the full nature and extent of the risks involved in an enterprise, suffers no actionable injury.[75] Drawing from *Munorwei v. Muza*,[76] the most relevant consideration when determining whether there is liability is a judicial officer's determination, based on his or her own notions of justice and fair play which are commonly informed by the general norms and sense of values generally prevailing in society, whether liability attaches or not.

62. Beyond just the athletes, it is also quite clear that liability can also extend to team personnel. For instance, team doctors could be liable for medical malpractice, a form of negligence, for giving a player a false clean bill of health just so that player may continue to perform. In all these instances, the team can also be jointly

70. *Donoghue v. Stevenson* (1932) UKHL 100.
71. (1985) 1 WLR 866.
72. *Condon v. Basi* (1985) 1 WLR 866.
73. Criminal Law (Codification and Reform) Act [Chapter 9:23].
74. *Caldwell v. Maguire and Fitzgerald* [2001] EWCA Civ 1054. *See also* Mark James & Fiona Deeley, *The Standard of Care in Sports Negligence Cases*, 1 Ent. & Sports L. J. 104–108 (2002).
75. *See Mutandiro*, *supra* n. 40. *Chipinge*, *supra* n. 41.
76. *Munorwei* (2015) ZWHHC 804. *See also Mutandiro, supra* n. 40.

liable unless it can show that it is exempt from liability. That is, this position at law is best illustrated by the approach adopted to the liability of personnel involved in an event by the Premier Soccer League (PSL). The PSL Rules and Regulations provide that all PSL Affiliated Clubs must ensure all soccer players are insured against injuries and losses and furnish the PSL with policy documents of the said policy before the commencement of each and every season.[77] Essentially, all persons involved can be liable. Indeed, the PSL Rules provide that any individual player, team or official who incites violence or who conducts himself in an ungentlemanly manner before, during and after the match shall be guilty of an offence and liable to be brought before the Disciplinary Committee for a hearing.[78] It is essential, therefore, for those governing sports to ensure that there are appropriate protections afforded to all those involved in sport.

II. Spectators

63. The actions of spectators, people who come to watch the sport, are also a matter of great public interest. Ideally, the involvement of spectators should extend only so far as appreciating the product before them. However, experience in Zimbabwe and other states has shown it to be the case that some spectators are so invested in the sport that they act in publicly deplorable ways meriting criminal or civil rebuke. And so, the criminal and civil liability that attaches to the actions of spectators is a quite important part of sports law.

64. The position in Zimbabwean law with respect to the conduct of spectators is that they always remain liable for the harm they cause. This is based on the law of delict which prescribes 'the circumstances in which one person can claim compensation from another for harm that has been suffered'.[79] Because it is not always easy to determine the spectator who causes harm or to prove that the accused spectator did in fact act as alleged, but it remains important to the public interest to ensure that those liable are held to account, Zimbabwean law imposes a duty of care on those event organisers to ensure that harm is averted. This is perhaps most reflected in the PSL Rules. The rules provide that no person shall bring alcohol into the stadium.[80] The sale of alcohol is strictly forbidden in any stadium before, during and after the match. The Home Team shall ensure that no alcohol is brought into the stadium by any spectator, official or player. Any breach of such will result in a fine as prescribed in the Standing Orders. Repeat offenders shall be summoned to a disciplinary hearing. The idea seems to be that spectators should be in full command of their senses at all times. In addition, the rules provide that the Home Team must ensure adequate security before any match occurs. Further, the Home Team shall be responsible for the behaviour of its spectators before, during and after the match until the stadium and its immediate surroundings are cleared of all persons. And, in

77. Order 27 of the Premier Soccer League (PSL) Rules and Regulations 2015 as amended.
78. Order 31 of the Premier Soccer League (PSL) Rules and Regulations 2015 as amended.
79. Loubser, *supra* n. 37.
80. Order 17.9 of the Premier Soccer League (PSL) Rules and Regulations 2015 as amended.

the event of any breach of peace occurring or any disturbance occurring within the stadium and among the spectators, this shall be subject to a disciplinary hearing. In sum, a team is responsible where it fails to provide adequate security at its venue; it shall be presumed, unless the contrary is proved, that a club has failed to provide adequate security at its venue where the spectators at such venue, irrespective of their affiliation, committed acts, or were responsible for conduct, which is considered improper behaviour. It shall not be a defence to the aforesaid charge that a larger crowd than anticipated attended or attempted to attend the game.

III. Sponsors

65. Sports have always generated enormous interest among the people of Zimbabwe. Such public interest has motivated different actors to sponsor sport for different reasons. Here, it is noteworthy that there have been difficulties in defining sports sponsorship itself and delimiting the groups of activities involved in it. This partly stems from popular confusion with such concepts as a charity, donation, endorsement and patronage. There does seem to be consensus, however, that sponsorship is really related to 'the acquisition of the rights to affiliate or directly associate with a product or event for the purpose of deriving benefits from that association'.[81] Separately, it has been described as 'the orchestration and implementation of marketing activities for the purpose of building and communicating an association (link) to a sponsorship'.[82] To this end, it can involve an investment in cash or kind in an activity, person or idea for the purpose of exploiting the potential associated with this activity.[83] It can also be the provision of resources by an organisation directly to an event or activity in exchange for a direct association with the event or activity.[84] The objective is often to enable the latter to pursue some activity in return for benefits contemplated in terms of the sponsor's promotion strategy, and which can be expressed in terms of corporate marketing or media objectives. As such, it is a business relationship that is based on an association between sponsors and sponsees with some promotional objectives in mind. In sports, the most common forms of sponsorship include: traditional sponsorship, which involves the acknowledgement of the sponsor by the sports property and the ability of the sponsor to use the property's trademarks and logos in its efforts to leverage the sponsorship and reinforce the relationship in the minds of members of the sponsor's

81. Bernard James Mullin, Stephen Hardy & William Anthony Sutton, *Sport Marketing* 254 (Human Kinetics 1993).
82. T. Bettina Cornwell & Isabelle Maignan, *An International Review of Sponsorship Research*, 93, 27 J. Advert. 1 (1998).
83. Tony Meenaghan, *The Role of Sponsorship in the Marketing Communications Mix*, 10 The Int'l J. Advert. (1991).
84. Dennis M. Sandler & David Shani, *Sponsorship and the Olympic Games: The Consumer Perspective*, 2 Sport Marketing Q. 38 (1993). Lesa Ukman, *IEG's Complete Guide to Sponsorship*, 154 (2004) defines sponsorship as 'a cash and/or in-kind fee paid to a property (typically sports, arts, entertainment, or causes) in return for access to the exploitable commercial potential associated with that property'.

target market; venue naming rights, which have often been characterised as building sponsorships where non-sports organisation are involved in the construction of sports facilities in return for the value that sponsors receive from stadium naming rights; endorsements, which involve the sponsorship of sports personalities by non-sports organisations in return for their endorsement of the sponsor's products; and licensing, which may involve giving sportswear manufacturing the right to use the logos of sports teams in the marketing of sportswear.

66. All this is noteworthy because research findings show that Zimbabwean companies are increasingly getting involved in sponsoring sports, though the extent of sponsorship is limited. There is a need to encourage greater sponsorship. To do so, it requires two things that are important to public regulation.

67. First, there is evidence to suggest that sponsors increasingly look to ensure that their final sponsorship selection is a well-informed business decision based on analysing the sponsee's potential to offer returns on their sponsorship investment. They prefer to associate with sports entities that can improve their brand equity, generate brand awareness, are compatible with their marketing objectives and relevant to the target audience. Thus, the increasing proportion of promotional budgets allocated to sponsorship has seen most companies trying to ensure that final sponsorship selection is a well-informed business decision and not 'a spur of the moment' agreement. Because of this, and the threat it poses to continued sponsorship, it is in the public interest, and thus a matter of public regulation, to ensure that sponsors have access to information and there is transparency in sponsorship. It is also a matter of public concern that sponsorship efforts are not abused or misappropriated, thus dissuading future sponsorship.[85] Depending on the nature of the offending act, a sponsor unlawfully claiming a tax break, a participant misappropriating sponsorship items, liability in Zimbabwe will be governed by the relevant aspect of the criminal law, most of which is contained and provided for in the Criminal Law (Codification and Reform) Act. In addition, a sponsor who suffers some harm can always rely on the law of delict which prescribes 'the circumstances in which one person can claim compensation from another for harm that has been suffered'[86] to hold the offending party liable, and thus get redress.

68. Second, the need to encourage sponsorship in sports, which is seen as a public good, has led to the adoption of the policy to exempt sponsors from paying taxes. Despite this being a public good, the fact that it is an exemption that removes money from the public coffers means that there is public interest in regulating these exemptions so that it is not an avenue that is abused by those looking to escape tax obligation.

---

85. Indeed, the Sports Commission's acting Director General Joseph Muchechetere has previously stated that there is need to up their game on issues to do with corporate governance. *See*, Chronicle Sport, *Muchechetere on Good Governance*, https://www.chronicle.co.zw/muchechetere-on-good-governance/ (accessed 18 Nov. 2019).
86. Loubser, *supra* n. 37.

IV. The General Public

69. The nature of public interest, and sometimes involvement, in sports means that there will be instances where members of the public, not directly involved in a sport, act in deplorable ways that offend the public interest and need to be regulated, such as poisoning a team's food in order to affect performance. Alternatively, there is public interest in ensuring that non-participants in sports do not get away with offensive acts such as negligently defaming participants. There is also public interest in ensuring that non-participants do not unlawfully benefit from exploiting the intellectual property of participants.

70. Significantly, whenever members of the public act in a manner that is untoward, as determined in the criminal law codified in the Criminal Law (Codification and Reform) Act or, as determined in civil law through mostly, but not exclusively, the common law, they will be liable criminally and civilly. It is also interesting to note that section 85(e) of the Constitution provides that any person acting in the public interest is entitled to approach a court, alleging that a fundamental right or freedom enshrined in the Constitution has been, is being or is likely to be infringed, and the court may grant appropriate relief, including a declaration of rights and an award of compensation. Because some fundamental rights such as the right to equality and the right to freedom of association are provided for in the Constitution, this provision empowers virtually any member of the public to bring a criminal or civil liability claim against any member of the public alleging that they are acting in a manner that compromises the integrity of sports.

§4. Tax

71. Experience has established that amateur and professional sports and the events around them often lead to the generation of significant revenues. These revenues emanate from several sources, including monies that are paid by sponsors. Revenues are also generated from the amounts remitted by the public when they pay to watch or participate in an event. Further, revenues are also generated by the associations. In addition to this, revenues generated filter down to several participants as wages. All this is significant because, in Zimbabwean law, all revenues generated are taxed and invested in community development and growing sport, and so, it is in the public interest that revenues are taxed.

72. Such taxation is based predominantly on the provisions in the ITA.[87] Section 8(1) of the ITA defines gross income as 'the total amount received by or accrued to or in favour of a person or deemed to have been received by or to have accrued to or in favour of a person in any year of assessment from a source within or deemed to be within Zimbabwe excluding any amount (not being any amount

87. Chapter 23:06.

included in "gross" income by virtue of any of the following paragraphs of this definition) so received or accrued which is proved by the taxpayer to be to be of capital nature'. Beyond this, the Act determines persons who are taxable.[88]

73. Effectively, the ITA essentially establishes that all participants in sports receiving an income from sport are liable to pay tax. Depending on the recipient of the income, such income assumes different forms. For leagues, income assumes the form of the sale of publication rights. To illustrate, television and radio rights for all matches of the PSL belong to the League and no matches may be televised or filmed without the consent of the League. In addition, the League may at its discretion levy a fee in respect of any team's entry into a particular cup tournament. Separately, for clubs, income assumes the form of subscription fees, admission fees, affiliation fees and registration of each team player. Insofar as players are concerned, income can assume the form of bonuses, allowances, signing fees received by sportsmen in the course of their employment ranks as salary. More recently, the growth of the gambling sector in Zimbabwe has been met with a state levy on all bookmakers that offer online sports betting. The levy collects 5% of gross earnings. The state has said the amounts levied will be used to enhance resources and upgrade any community sports within the country. And so, the main goal of the new levy is not to punish those that are engaging in sports betting but to generate revenue to help with the growth of sports in the country. It has been suggested that the revenue that is generated will also help create and maintain a recreation infrastructure.[89]

74. The general position in sports is for the employer to withdraw tax contributions from the employee salaries and remit these to the revenue authority. Where an athlete generates revenue from international competition or from activities in which the athlete does not partake as an employee, it falls to the athlete to ensure that she or he remits the necessary amounts to the revenue authority. And expectedly, in terms of the ITA, the failure to remit the amount, or the right amount, is a criminal offence.

§5. Sports Justice

75. The preamble to the Constitution suggests, in part, that Zimbabweans are united in a desire to banish injustice. Insofar as sport is concerned, the sheer number of participants involved in sport in Zimbabwe means that it is inevitable that conflicts, disputes, and injustices, whether perceived or real, will occur. And so, between the Constitution and the need to ensure that injustices, whether perceived or real, are addressed, securing sports justice is in the public interest.

---

88. Section 2 of ITA defines a person in addition to the ordinary meaning of a natural individual person as a company, a local like authority, a deceased or insolvent estate, in relation to income, the subject of trust to which no beneficiary is entitled.
89. Agencies, *What the Sports Betting Levy Means for Zimbabwe Sports*, https://bulawayo24.com/index-id-sports-sc-local-byo-139456.html (accessed 20 Mar. 2020).

76. Essentially, the most common method of securing such justice is through ensuring access to dispute resolution which is non-confrontational but looks to achieve conciliatory outcomes. To this end, the SRC Act asserts that sports associations should have Constitutions that provide for dispute resolution. Importantly, though, there is no central dispute resolution body charged with the responsibility of adjudicating all sports-related matters at a private level. And to date, not all the sports have put in place dispute resolution bodies charged with ensuring that there is justice, real and perceived. Sports such as boxing, tennis, rugby and athletics do not have internal judicial bodies. However, the situation is different with the more popular sports like football and cricket. In addition to this, the 2013 SRC Charter on Cooperate Governance advocates the turn to non-confrontational methods of dispute resolution to be adopted by the NSA.

77. Where justice issues surround employment issues, the position is that a participant in sports with a labour dispute or labour-related matter may refer the matter to the Ministry of Labour, where it will be dealt with by a Labour Officer and thereafter by a senior labour officer. Importantly, in terms of section 94 of the Labour Act, no Labour Officer shall entertain any dispute or unfair labour practice unless it is referred to him or her or has otherwise come to his or her attention within two years from the date when the dispute or unfair labour practice first arose. However, if a dispute or unfair labour practice is continuing at the time it is referred to or comes to the attention of the Labour Officer, the prescription period is irrelevant and the Labour Officer must entertain the dispute or unfair labour practice regardless of the length of time it has been there. In addition, sections 93–94 of the Labour Act direct the labour officers to rely on a number of non-confrontational methods of dispute resolution such as conciliation/mediation,[90] collective bargaining, and arbitration, as precursors turn to the more adversarial methods such as adjudication and collective job action. In addition to this, however, the law reserves access to justice in more traditional, and adversarial, fora such as the Constitutional Court, the Supreme Court, the High Court, the Administrative Court, the Labour Court and the Magistrates' Courts.[91] This is a matter explored in greater detail when dispute resolution in sports is discussed in the ensuing sections.

---

90. Both conciliation and mediation refer to a procedure where a third party assists parties in the course of negotiations or when negotiations have reached deadlock, to facilitate agreement on the issues in dispute. The difference between the two systems depends on the degree of participation of the third party.
91. Pfumorodze & Chitsove, *supra* n. 25.

Part II. Sport and Employment

Chapter 1. General Issues

78. There is an extremely wide range of participants involved in sports, including the leadership, players and clubs, local, national and international organisations, spectators, the media, commercial and non-commercial interests, and educational and training bodies. Most of these participants are involved in some sort of employment relationship with each other.[92] And crucially, this is a relationship that can easily be exploited based on whoever holds power at the time of contracting, culminating in unfair labour practices which run contrary to the public interest which is an untenable state of affairs.

79. It is no wonder then that Zimbabwean law, which is found in several sources, most notably, the Constitution, legislation, the common law, judicial precedent, and authoritative texts, looks to closely regulate employment so that the public interest is protected. To this end, section 14 of the Zimbabwean Constitution provides that the state and all institutions and agencies of government at every level must endeavour to facilitate and take measures to empower, through appropriate, transparent, fair and just affirmative action, all marginalised persons, groups and communities in Zimbabwe. Further, at all times, the state and all institutions and agencies of government at every level must ensure that appropriate and adequate measures are undertaken to create employment for all Zimbabweans, especially women and youths. In complement to this, section 17 of the Constitution provides that the state must promote full gender balance in Zimbabwean society, and in particular: the state must promote the full participation of women in all spheres of Zimbabwean society on the basis of equality with men; the state must take all measures, including legislative measures, needed to ensure that both genders are equally represented in all institutions and agencies of government at every level; and civil service recruitment women constitute at least half the membership of all Commissions and other elective and appointed governmental bodies established by or under this Constitution or any Act of Parliament; the state and all institutions and agencies of government at every level must take practical measures to ensure that women have access to resources, including land, on the basis of equality with men. The state must also take positive measures to rectify gender discrimination and imbalances resulting from

92. Most of the participants are not employees, and there tends to be a distinction between professional sportspersons and those that are not professionals. Due to the nature of sports, this distinction is sometimes difficult and some athletes may not be considered employees.

past practices and policies. In addition, section 24 provides that the state and all institutions and agencies of government at every level must adopt reasonable policies and measures, within the limits of the resources available to them, to provide everyone with an opportunity to work in a freely chosen activity, in order to secure a decent living for themselves and their families. The state and all institutions and agencies of government at every level are also directed to endeavour to secure: full employment; the removal of restrictions that unnecessarily inhibit or prevent people from working and otherwise engaging in gainful economic activities; vocational guidance and the development of vocational and training programmes, including those for persons with disabilities; and the implementation of measures such as family care that enable women to enjoy a real opportunity to work. Beyond this, section 54 of the Constitution provides that no person may be subjected to slavery or servitude and section 55 that no person may be made to perform forced or compulsory labour. In addition, section 59 provides that every person has the right to demonstrate and to present petitions, but these rights must be exercised peacefully. And, in section 64, every person has the right to choose and carry on any profession, trade or occupation, but the practice of a profession, trade or occupation may be regulated by law. Section 65 expands on all this and provides a more detailed account of labour rights. To this end, section 65 provides that every person has the right to fair and safe labour practices and standards and to be paid a fair and reasonable wage. The section also provides that except for members of the security services, every person has the right to form and join trade unions and employee or employers' organisations of their choice and to participate in the lawful activities of those unions and organisations. And further, except for members of the security services, every employee has the right to participate in collective job action, including the right to strike, sit in, withdraw their labour and take other similar concerted action, but a law may restrict the exercise of this right in order to maintain essential services. And every employee is entitled to just, equitable and satisfactory conditions of work. Further, except for members of the security services, every employee, employer, trade union, and employee or employer's organisation has the right to: engage in collective bargaining; organise; and form and join federations of such unions and organisations. Importantly, section 65 provides that women and men have a right to equal remuneration for similar work. In addition, women employees have a right to fully paid maternity leave for a period of at least three months.

80. While these provisions in the Constitution form the backbone of the employment law framework in Zimbabwe, the finer aspects of employment law are extensively regulated by dedicated employment legislation, most notably, the Labour Act which, generally, dictates that formal employment relationships should be established, managed, and terminated in ways that are consistent with its provisions.[93] These provisions include, for instance, the requirement that contracts should feature express terms that establish the nature of the employment relationship such that whatever is written in a contract will be relied on in establishing the duties and

93. Also note, s. 3(1) of this Act creates a two-tier labour law system in Zimbabwe and in that the Labour Act only applies to employees and employers in the private sector, local authorities, state universities and parastatals. Civil servants are covered by the Public Service Act.

rights of the contracting parties. Notably, the Act only applies to employees as defined in section 2 of the Act. It does not apply to independent contractors. And, it is with respect to these employees that section 12(3) of the Act provides that 'a contract of employment that does not specify its duration or date of termination, other than a contract for casual work or seasonal work or for the performance of some specific service, shall be deemed to be a contract without limit of time'. However, there is the proviso that 'a casual worker shall be deemed to have become an employee on a contract of employment without limit of time on the day that his period of engagement with a particular employer exceeds a total of six weeks in any four consecutive months'. Effectively, the Act draws a distinction between casual or seasonal workers, employees on a fixed-term contract, and employees on a contract with a limit of time.

81. According to section 2 of the Act, casual work is work for which an employee is engaged by an employer for not more than a total of six weeks in any four consecutive months. Importantly, once a contract for casual work exceeds the prescribed period of a total of six weeks in any four consecutive months, it is deemed to have become a contract of employment without a limit of time.[94] Alternatively, seasonal work means work that is, owing to the nature of the industry, performed only at certain times of the year. Separately, section 12(2)(b) notes that fixed-term contracts arise where the employer provides written particulars of the period of time, if limited, for which the employee is engaged. Importantly, and as noted previously, in *UZ-UCSF Collaborative Research Programme in Women's Health v. Shamuyarira*, the Supreme Court held that the continued renewal of fixed-term contracts over a period of time does not create a legitimate expectation of re-employment or permanent employment. Further to this, section 12(4a) of the Labour Act provides that 'no employer shall terminate a contract of employment on notice unless the termination is in terms of an employment code or, in the absence of an employment code, in terms of the model code made under section 101(9); or the employer and employee mutually agree in writing to the termination of the contract or; the employee was engaged for a period of fixed duration or for the performance of some specific service; or pursuant to retrenchment'. It is also worth noting here that in addition to all this, section 17 of the Act empowers the Minister to promulgate regulations covering virtually every aspect of the employment relationship. Regulations made in terms of this section 'override every contract, agreement, arrangement of any kind whatsoever, determination or regulation made in terms of any enactment which related to the employment of an employee … ' to the extent of any inconsistency.

82. Beyond this, and consistent with the 'presumption against alteration in the common law by statute law unless the words of the statute are plain and unambiguous and an intention to later the common law is evident from the wording of the enactment … if the arguments on a question of interpretation are fairly evenly balanced, that interpretation should be adopted which involves the least alteration of

94. *Simbi*, *supra* n. 15.

the common law',[95] it is worth noting that employment relationships are also governed by the common law. This body of law provides that employment contracts, as with any other contracts, are valid when certain elements are present such as the agreement has to be lawful, with the real possibility of performance, among parties with contractual capacity, holding a real intent to contract, who abide by the formalities that attach to the relevant contracts.[96] Beyond this, the common law also provides that in order for a contract to materialise, an offer must be made to one person or the public[97] which is consistent with all the essentials of the contract.[98] Following this, an offeree must accept the offer within a prescribed or reasonable time[99] and communicate this in clear terms to the offeror.[100] Of note, revocation of an offer is quite acceptable.[101] However, revocation is not effective until the offeree is aware of it. And so, an offer can be revoked at any stage before it is accepted as long as the offeror takes reasonable steps to find and inform the offeree of the revocation.[102] And so, while the Labour Act may be comprehensive in its coverage of employment law, any gaps that remain are governed by the common law. For instance, while section 12(4) of the Labour Act governs the time periods that apply when a contract of employment is terminated on notice at the instance of either the employer or employee, the Act does not define the term resignation. Instead, it is left to the courts, using the common law, to establish the actual definition and scope of the term 'resignation'. Here, it is worth restating that the Supreme Court in *Madondo v. Conquip Zimbabwe (Pvt) Ltd*[103] noted that a resignation is an act of giving up one's job or position on notice or without notice.[104] And so, when gaps manifest, the common law simply kicks in. This is also true with respect to breach of contract. For instance, in *Guthrie Zhokinyi v. Dynamos*,[105] the Labour Court ruled that despite being banned by ZIFA, Dynamos had not terminated his contract so it remained in operation. He continued offering his services to the club but the club just ignored him. Dynamos argued that the ban rendered him incompetent to render any service as to any employer and that there was no reason for formal termination of contract.

95. *Hama, supra* n. 26, at 664.
96. *Southampton, supra* n. 27, at 12. *Jordan, supra* n. 27, at 825.
97. *Carlill, supra* n. 28, at 256.
98. *Green Acres, supra* n. 29, at 17.
99. *Boyd, supra* n. 30, at 414.
100. *Levenstein, supra* n. 31, at 615. *Bloom, supra* n. 31, at 100.
101. *Bryne, supra* n. 32, at 344.
102. *Ibid.*
103. *Madondo v. Conquip Zimbabwe (Pvt) Ltd* SC 25/16.
104. Kasuso, *supra* n. 35, at 3.
105. Staff Reporter, *supra* n. 36.

Chapter 2. Employment and the Sports Law in Zimbabwe

83. It is within the context of the above general position that employment relationships in sports are regulated. Because there is no dedicated body of sports law, it is a version of the law discussed above, focusing on issues relevant to sports, that constitutes the sports law on employment in Zimbabwe. This part of the monograph is dedicated to discussing three issues that are particularly important in sports and employment, that is the general position of the law on sports and employment, the legal position on the lawful resolution of disputes, and the role that law plays in looking to secure the social welfare of participants.

§1. Sports Employment Law in Zimbabwe

84. From the amalgam of constitutional provisions, provisions in the Labour Act, and common law principles that make up the employment law in Zimbabwe, it is possible to establish that there are fundamental pillars of sports employment law in Zimbabwe.

85. First, with respect to participation in sports, it is quite clear that the law looks to ensure that participation is open to everyone. To this end, the state has an obligation to ensure that such participation is realised in meaningful ways. And, there can be no discrimination in sports. If anything, there is a need for affirmative action. In addition to this, it is also worth noting with respect to participation in sport that section 19(3) of the Constitution enjoins the state to take appropriate legislative and other measures to protect children from exploitative labour practices, ensure that children are not required or permitted to perform work or provide services that are inappropriate for the children's age, or place the children's well-being, education, physical or mental health or spiritual, moral or social development at risk. This is supported by section 11(1) of the Labour Act which provides that no employer shall employ any person in any occupation as an apprentice who is under the age of 13 years, otherwise than as an apprentice who is under the age of 15 years.

86. Further, section 11(2) of the Labour Act provides that any contract of employment entered in contravention of subsection (1), and any contract of apprenticeship with an apprentice between the ages of 13 and 15 years which was entered without the assistance of the apprentice's guardian, shall be void and unenforceable against the person purportedly employed under such contract, whether or not (in the case of a contravention of paragraph (b) of subsection (1)) such person was assisted by his guardian, or was married or otherwise tacitly or expressly emancipated, but such person may enforce any rights that have accrued to him by or under such contract. Section 11(3) goes further to provide that a person under the age of 15 years but not younger than 13 years may perform work at a school or technical or vocational institution that is carried out as an integral part of a course of training or technical or vocational education for which the school or institution is primarily responsible; and perform work in an undertaking that is carried out in conjunction with a course of technical or vocational education.

87. In addition, section 11(4) provides that no employer shall cause any person under the age of 18 years to perform any work which is likely to jeopardise that person's health, safety or morals, which work shall include but not be limited to work involving such activities as may be prescribed. And section 11(5) provides that any employer who employs any person in contravention of subsection (1) or (4) shall be guilty of an offence and liable to a fine not exceeding ZWL 30,000 or to imprisonment not exceeding two years or both fine and imprisonment.

88. Importantly, though, section 60(3) of the Constitution provides that guardians have the right to determine, in accordance with their beliefs, the moral and religious upbringing of their children, provided they do not prejudice the rights to which their children are entitled under this Constitution, including their rights to education, health, safety and welfare. In addition to this, section 20 of the Constitution provides that the state and all institutions and agencies of government at every level must take reasonable measures, including affirmative action programmes, to ensure that youths, that is to say, people between the ages of 15 and 35 years, have access to appropriate education and training; have opportunities to associate and be represented and participate in political, social, economic and other spheres of life; are afforded opportunities for employment and other avenues to economic empowerment; have opportunities for recreational activities and access to recreational facilities; and are protected from harmful cultural practices, exploitation and all forms of abuse.

89. Hence, the position on minors' participation in employment relationships in sports law in Zimbabwe is that, while minors require protection from unfair labour practices, they can also be amateur or professional sportspersons and, thus, employees as long as they are assisted in contracting by an empowered guardian.[106] The practical application of all this is apparent from the PSL Rules and Regulations which provide that no club may enter into a contract with a player who is a minor unless he is assisted by either a parent or a guardian.[107] Such consent shall be evidenced by the parent or guardian countersigning the said contract, which will be invalid in the absence of such countersignature. A player who has not yet reached his 18th birthday may sign a contract as a non-amateur only for a period not exceeding three years.[108]

90. Second, the sports law is quite clear in prescribing the form that employment contracts must assume. To this end, Zimbabwean sports law requires contracts to be in written form and expressing the rights and duties of parties to the contract.[109] And, even when this is not the case, the sports law establishes clear duties that fall to employers. To this end, the law establishes that, regardless of the terms

---

106. *Edelstein v. Edelstein* N.O. 1952 (3) S.A. 1 (A.D.).
107. PSL, *Premier Soccer League Rules and Regulations*, Order 3.5., http://www.fuz.co.zw/statutes/0-1522155406PSL%20Rules%20and%20Regulations%20Final.pdf (accessed 2 Mar. 2020).
108. PSL, *supra* n. 107, at Order 3.5.
109. *See* s. 12(2) of the Labour Act.

in a contract, the most fundamental duty of the employment contract is that employers must remunerate employees.[110] This duty, which can be executed daily, weekly, fortnightly or monthly, arises from the tendering of service and not from the actual performance of work. The logic here is that employers should not unjustly enrich themselves at the expense of employees by refusing to pay for the services rendered to them from which they have benefited.[111] However, where the employee is unavailable to tender service, the club is not obliged to pay. This position, traceable to the common law, is recognised in section 12A of the Labour Act which requires players to be paid their remuneration in cash.[112] It has been accepted, however, that remuneration may partly be paid in kind where this has been part of custom and practice. In addition, an employer may not unilaterally deduct any amount from the remuneration to which the employee is entitled unless the employee has agreed to this in respect of a specific debt, or unless deductions are required or permitted in terms of the law, collective agreement, court order or arbitral award. Quite related to this, employers also have a duty to provide employees with work. Here, it is important to note that it is well within a club's remit to let the player sit and do nothing as long as the player receives his or her due remuneration.[113] However, employers' and clubs included have taken the above reasoning of the court to mean that if they force an employee or a player into idleness, by giving less work or no work to do at all, it would be cheaper than dismissal. These circumstances are similar to the circumstances in *Kandembiri v. Director of DDF and Another*, where the employer decided not to give work to a driver who had been involved in an accident with a company vehicle, ostensibly as a way of frustrating him. However, the employer continued to pay his wages. When the driver stopped coming to work, he was dismissed.[114] The High Court upheld the dismissal as lawful. However, it was held that there are exceptions to this. In instances where remuneration is based on the performance done or where the failure to allow the player to have game time degrades his status, or where the club has contracted to train the employee in a particular profession or trade as in the case, for example, of articled clerks and apprentices, the employer has a duty to provide actual work. Separately, the Supreme Court has argued that 'an employer who had rendered a reinstated employee idle was in breach of contract because the employee's remuneration depended on actual work'.[115]

91. Third, sports employment law in Zimbabwe regulates different categories of employee-employer relationships. For instance, while no formal distinction is drawn between the two, Zimbabwean sports law recognises, and treats differently, 'professional' and 'amateur' athletes. From the preceding discussion, it is easy to see how this distinction is important in law because an amateur athlete is one who has no written contract and earns less than what he or she usually spends in order to practise a particular sport. And so, players who have never received any remuneration other than reimbursement of their actual expenses incurred during the course of

110. *Brown v. Hicks* 1902 19 SC 314 at 315.
111. *City of Harare v. Zimuch* 1995 (1) ZLR 285.
112. Labour Act [Chapter 28: 01].
113. *Commercial Careers College (1980) (Pvt) Ltd v. Jarvis* 1989 (1) ZLR 344 (SC) at 350G-351B.
114. HH-6-98.
115. *Standard Chartered Bank of Zimbabwe Ltd v. Matsika* 1997 (2) ZLR 389.

their participation in a sport or event are regarded as amateurs. Indeed, the PSL Rules and Regulations[116] serve as a good example here because they apply to soccer, one of the most popular and regulated sporting disciplines in Zimbabwe, note that 'players who have never received any remuneration other than reimbursement of their actual expenses incurred during the course of their participation in or any activity connected with association football are regarded as amateurs'. The rules go further to note that travel and hotel expenses incurred through involvement in a match and the costs of player's equipment, insurance and training may be reimbursed without jeopardising a player's amateur status.[117]

92. Conversely, it is widely accepted that a professional player is one who has a written contract and spends less than what he or she is paid in order to practise a particular sport. To this end, any player who has never received any remuneration other than reimbursement of their actual expenses incurred during the course of their participation in a sport or event is a professional athlete. To illustrate, the PSL Rules cited above note that any person who has received remuneration in excess of the amount stated under these regulations in respect of participation in or any activity connected with association football shall be regarded as a professional unless he has reacquired the amateur status.[118] Further, such a player should have a written contract and the club should provide him or her with a duly certified copy of the contract upon thereof by the club that signs him. Such contracts shall be financial contracts concluded for a minimum duration of one year, a maximum duration of five years, or any other period as prescribed by the FIFA Regulations on Transfer of Players.[119] Importantly, a copy of these contracts shall be provided to the League in a sealed envelope attached to the registration form having been signed and, upon demand, made available to ZIFA or FIFA. The sealed envelope containing the contracts may be opened only in the presence of the CEO, or a person or subcommittee designated by the League. If the parties agree to terminate a contract before the stipulated date, they shall notify the CEO of the League thereof in writing within fourteen days of the agreement having been reached.[120] Of course, where the person is an employee in terms of the Labour Act, termination must comply with the Act.

93. Separately, another employee-employer relationship that is canvassed by sports law in Zimbabwe is the relationship that exists between leagues and persons assuming the roles of referees and umpires. These people serve essential roles in any sport or event and they are of particular interest because they ensure fairness and adherence to the rules. However, their role means that they cannot be employed by the teams or clubs. Importantly, because they are not employees, they are not afforded protections reserved for employees under the Act. The way around this has

116. PSL, *supra* n. 107, at Order 2.2.
117. PSL, *supra* n. 107, at Order 2.3.
118. PSL, *supra* n. 107.
119. PSL, *supra* n. 107, at Order 3.2.
120. PSL, *supra* n. 107, at Order 3.4.

been to ensure that the associations governing a particular sport ensure that they register enough qualified referees, though these referees are not employees of the associations in which they are recognised but are regarded as independent contractors. In the PSL Rules, for instance, referees for league matches and tournaments under the PSL jurisdiction are appointed by the ZIFA Referees Appointment Committee from a national list compiled by the ZIFA Referees Committee.[121] The Referees Appointments Committee shall be a subcommittee appointed by the ZIFA Executive Committee in terms of the ZIFA Statutes.

94. In addition to all this, Zimbabwean sports law, like the laws of several other states across the world, also regulates contractual relationships which are not traditional employer-employee relationships. For instance, it is well established that boxers negotiate their own transactions with respect to whom to fight and when to fight. This effectively means that the boxer is not an employee but is guided in making decisions by a promoter and a coach. In terms of Zimbabwean sports law, when they act in this way, these promoters and coaches are best regarded as agents of the boxer. Agents act as intermediaries between sportspersons and sports clubs/organisers of sports events with a view to employing the sportspersons.[122] Agents also find job placements for sportspersons. In addition, Agents can be engaged to conclude different kinds of contracts on behalf of the sportsperson or managing the assets of the sportsperson. Outstandingly, there are no laws dedicated to the regulation of the activities of sports agents. However, being agents, their conduct is regulated in terms of the common law, which recognises agency. In addition, the conduct of agents is also regulated by several international institutions such as FIFA, WA, and Rugby Union, which have prescribed rules which regulate the conduct of agents. These rules are applied in Zimbabwe by subsidiaries to international institutions such as ZIFA, the PSL, NAAZ, and Rugby Zimbabwe. For instance, Order 7.6 of the PSL Rules provides that 'players and clubs are forbidden from using the services of non-licensed Players' Agents'. However, the ban does not apply if the agent acting on behalf of a player, sibling or the spouse of the player in question or if the agent acting on behalf of the player or club is legally authorised to practise as a lawyer in compliance with the rules in force in his country of domicile.[123]

§2. Dispute Resolution in Sports

95. Disputes inevitably arise. Where they do, in order to protect industrial relationships from anarchy and preserving industrial peace, the Labour Act in Part XII

121. PSL, *supra* n. 107, at Order 21.1.
122. European Commission, *European Commission's White Paper on Sport*, 11 July 2007, COM (2007) 391, https://eur-lex.europa.eu/legal-content/EN/TXT/?uri=CELEX%3A52007DC0391 (accessed 20 Mar. 2020).
123. PSL, *supra* n. 107, at Order 7.7.

establishes structures and processes of dispute resolution.[124] The various methods of dispute resolution established by labour legislation are comprehensively discussed by Kasuso who notes that dispute resolution can assume three different forms depending on the circumstances. First, the Labour Act provides a framework for conciliation of industrial disputes in section 93(1) of the Act by providing that 'A labour officer to whom a dispute has been referred, or to whose attention it has come, shall attempt to settle it through conciliation or, if agreed by the parties, by reference to arbitration.' Importantly, the Labour Act does not define the term 'conciliation' but it is understood as a process involving assisting the parties to clarify their points of disagreement and attempting to promote a settlement but the terms of any settlement remain the responsibility of the parties. Because section 93(1) of the Labour Act is worded in peremptory terms, conciliation is mandatory unless the parties have referred their dispute to voluntary arbitration. Conciliation is done by Labour Officers who are employed by the State and have national jurisdiction. In the National Employment Councils, conciliation is done by Designated Agents and their jurisdiction is limited to a given industry or undertaking. Both disputes of interest and disputes of rights are subject to conciliation. At conciliation, the Labour Officer does not adjudicate a dispute but carries out an enquiry and attempts to have the parties reach an amicable settlement. In the event that the parties do not reach an agreement, the Labour Officer can still try to re-engage the parties. However, the conciliation process is given a time span of thirty days from the day the Labour Officer begins the process.[125] This period can be extended to a maximum of ninety days subject to the agreement of the parties in terms of section 3(5) of the Labour (Settlement of Disputes) Regulations, 2003. If the dispute is not resolved within the thirty-day period or the extended ninety-day period, a Labour Officer must bring the process of conciliation to an end, and issue a certificate of no settlement (section 93(3) of the Labour Act) which must be signed by the Labour Officer. In terms of section 93(5) of the Labour Act as amended by the Labour (Amendment) Act 5 of 2015:

> (5) After a labour officer has issued a certificate of no settlement, the labour officer, upon consulting any labour officer who is senior to him or her and to whom he or she is responsible in the area in which he or she attempted to settle the dispute of unfair labour practice –
>
> (a) shall refer the dispute to compulsory arbitration if the dispute is a dispute of interest and the parties are engaged in an essential service, and the provisions of section 98 shall apply to such reference to compulsory arbitration.
>
> (b) may, with the agreement of the parties, refer the dispute or unfair labour practice to voluntary arbitration if the dispute is a dispute of interest, or
>
> (c) may if the dispute or unfair labour practice is a dispute of right;

124. These are complemented by the following pieces of legislation: Arbitration Act (Chapter 7:15), Administrative Justice Act (Chapter 10:28), the Labour (Settlement of Disputes) Regulations, 2003 and the Labour Court Rules, 2017.

125. Section 93(8) of the Labour Act.

make a ruling that; upon finding on a balance of probabilities that-

(i) the employer or other person is guilty of an unfair labour practice; or

(ii) the dispute of right or unfair labour practice must be resolved against any employer or other person in a specific manner by an order –

A. Directing the employee or other party concerned to cease or rectify the infringement or threatened infringement, as the case may be, including the payment of moneys, where appropriate;

B. For damages for any loss or prospective loss caused either directly or indirectly, as a result of the infringement or threatened infringement, as the case may be;

whereupon the provisions of subsections (5a) and (5b) shall apply.

96. In the event of failure of conciliation and after the issuance of a certificate of no settlement, a Labour Officer has the following options. First, he or she shall refer the dispute to compulsory arbitration on the condition that the dispute is a dispute of interest. In addition, the parties must be those engaged in an essential service. Section 102 of the Labour Act defines essential services and the Labour (Declaration of Essential Services) Notice 137 of 2003 lists the following services as essential services: fire brigade, distribution of water, veterinary services, services provided by revenue specialists, health services, transport and communication services, electricity services and any public broadcaster among others. The framework for compulsory arbitration is provided in section 98 of the Labour Act. Second, the Labour Officer may, with the agreement of the parties, refer the dispute to voluntary arbitration. Third, the Labour Officer may, if the dispute or unfair labour practice is a dispute of right, proceed to make a ruling. In this scenario, the Labour Officer is no longer a conciliator but an adjudicator. Once a ruling has been made, section 93(5a) of the Labour Act as amended is invoked.[126] And, in *Drum City (Pvt) Ltd v. Garudzo* SC 57/18, section 93(5a) of the Labour Act was interpreted to entail the following:

(a) The Labour Officer, after making a ruling in terms of section 93(5)(c)(ii) of the Act, makes an affidavit to that effect and attaches to it any evidence on which such ruling is based.

(b) The Labour Officer then gives notice to the employer or any person against whom such ruling and order is made (respondent), of the lodging by him, of an application with the Labour Court for an order directing the respondent to comply with the ruling within a period not less than thirty days from the date the matter is set down for hearing (restitution day).

(c) The Labour Officer then appears before the Labour Court on the date of the hearing, as the applicant, seeking an order confirming his or her draft ruling.

126. Tapiwa G. Kasuso, *Labour Law Zimbabwe Open University Labour Law Module* (2019).

(d) Should the respondent fail to make an appearance, the Labour Court will nevertheless make a ruling confirming the order with or without an amendment.
(e) On the date of the hearing (and presumably with the respondent in attendance), the Labour Court may also conduct a hearing and grant (confirm) the order sought with or without amendment.
(f) Thereafter, should the respondent fail to comply with the order of the Labour Court within thirty days of the hearing date, the Labour Officer will submit to the relevant court, such order for registration.
(g) Upon submission of the order to the relevant court for registration, it shall have the same effect for purposes of enforcement, as any civil judgment of that court.

It must be noted that only if the Labour Officer rules against the employer or any person will he or she be required to take the ruling for confirmation to the Labour Court. Once the ruling is confirmed, it can then be registered with either the High Court or Magistrates' Court for enforcement purposes.[127]

97. Second, the Labour Act provides for voluntary arbitration and compulsory arbitration. To this end, voluntary arbitration arises under section 93(1) where parties may agree to forego conciliation and opt for voluntary arbitration. Alternatively, in terms of section 93(b) of the Labour Act, parties may agree after the issuance of a certificate of no settlement by a Labour Officer to refer their dispute to voluntary arbitration. The common denominator in both instances is that this form of arbitration arises from the agreement of the parties. Importantly, voluntary arbitration is not governed by the Labour Act, but by the Arbitration Act.[128]In conclusion of the arbitration proceedings, the arbitrator hands down an award in writing, with reasons upon which it is based. The award can thereafter be enforced by registering it with either the Magistrates' Court or High Court depending on its monetary value. A party aggrieved by a decision of an arbitrator in voluntary arbitration can only challenge the award by making an application for the setting aside of the award in the High Court. The application is made in terms of Article 34 of the Model Law to the Arbitration Act. In addition, a voluntary arbitration award can only be set aside on the basis of the grounds in Article 34(2) of the Model Law to the Arbitration Act which include, among others, a party to the arbitration agreement lacked capacity, no proper notice of appointment of the arbitrator and arbitral proceedings was given; award dealt with a dispute which cannot be subject to arbitration and the award is against public policy. With respect to compulsory arbitration, this is only available after the failure of conciliation and the issuing of a certificate of no settlement in terms of section 93(5) (a) of the Labour Act. The dispute must be a dispute of interest and the parties must be engaged in an essential service. In terms of section 98(11) of the Labour Act, once a dispute of interest has been referred to for compulsory arbitration, no collective job action in respect of the dispute may be engaged in. The procedure in compulsory arbitration is regulated in section 98 of the Labour Act. In terms of section 98(3) of the Labour Act, before a

127. Kasuso, *supra* n. 126.
128. Chapter 7:15.

dispute is referred to as compulsory arbitration, parties must be afforded an opportunity to make representations, especially on terms of reference. The parties do not choose an arbitrator, but the Labour Officer appoints an arbitrator from a list of arbitrators prepared by the Minister of Labour (section 98(5) of the Labour Act). The annual appointment, fees to be charged and ethical conduct of these arbitrators are regulated by the Labour (Arbitrators) Regulations, 2012. Section 98(2) of the LA provides that any matters not covered by section 98 of the Act in respect of arbitration proceedings are regulated by the Arbitration Act. For instance, the conduct of the hearing and making of an award are issues not covered by the Labour Act, and in such situations, the Arbitration Act applies. To enforce an arbitral award made under section 98 of the Labour Act, a party to whom it relates must submit it for registration to the Magistrates' Court or High Court depending on the quantum of the award (sections 14 and 15 of the Labour Act). Importantly, an arbitral award made under compulsory arbitration can only be challenged in the Labour Court on appeal only on questions of law.[129]

98. Third, dispute resolution can be led by the Labour Court which was established in March 2003 by the Labour Relations (Amendment) Act 17 of 2002 (Amendment Act, 2002) to replace what was formerly the Labour Relations Tribunal and was established in section 83(1) of the Labour Relations Act. And so, unlike other superior courts, the Labour Court was not provided for under the 1980 Constitution. However, section 162 of Zimbabwe's 2013 Constitution provides that judicial authority in Zimbabwe is vested in the following courts: the Constitutional Court, the Supreme Court, the High Court, the Labour Court, the Administrative Court, Magistrates' Courts, customary law and local courts and other courts established by or under an Act of Parliament. Since then, section 5 of the Constitution of Zimbabwe (Amendment) (No. 1) Act 2017 has clarified that 'For the purpose of this section and section 171(1)(b), it is declared, for the avoidance of doubt, that the Labour Court and Administrative Court are courts subordinate to the High Court.' Importantly, the Labour Court's functions, powers and jurisdiction are circumscribed in section 89(1) and 89(6) of the Labour Act which provides as follows:

(1) The Labour Court shall exercise the following functions –
- (a) hearing and determining applications and appeals in terms of this Act or any other enactment;
- (b) hearing and determining matters referred to it by the Minister in terms of this Act;
- (c) referring a dispute to a labour officer, designated agent or a person appointed by the Labour Court to conciliate the dispute if the Labour Court considers it expedient to do so;
- (d) appointing an arbitrator from the panel of arbitrators referred to in subsection (6) of section ninety-eight to hear and determine an application;

129. Tapiwa G. Kasuso, *Resignation of an Employee under Zimbabwean Labour Law*, 4 Midlands State U. L. Rev. 3 (2017). *Zimbabwe Education Scientific, Social and Cultural Workers Union v. Welfare Educational Employers Institutions Association* SC11/13, *Mhisva v. Rainbow Tourism Group Ltd* 2009 (2) ZLR 33 (S).

(d1)exercise the same powers of review as would be exercisable by the High Court in respect of labour matters;

(e) doing such other things as may be assigned to it in terms of this Act or any other enactment.

(6) No court, other than the Labour Court, shall have jurisdiction in the first instance to hear and determine any application, appeal or matter referred to in subsection (1).

Also important, the Labour Court was deprived of the competence and power to enforce its own judgments. As such, a successful litigant must approach the traditional civil courts and register a Labour Court order for enforcement purposes. The registration is purely an administrative process on the part of the registering court which does not sit as a review or appeal court with jurisdiction to question the Labour Court decision.[130] It is worth noting, however, that the Constitution establishes the Supreme Court as the final Court of Appeal in respect of all disputes which do not raise constitutional matters, including labour matters. And, section 92F(1) of the Labour Act provides that an appeal on a question of law only shall lie to the Supreme Court from any decision of the Labour Court.[131] A party seeking to appeal against a Labour Court determination must also obtain leave to appeal from the Judge or Judges of the Labour Court who made the decision. In the absence of the Judge, leave can be sought from any Judge of the Labour Court. If leave is refused, section 92F(3) of the Labour Act allows a party to seek leave from a Judge of the Supreme Court.[132] Lastly, appeals always lie to the Constitutional Court where labour disputes relate to a constitutional matter.[133] Obviously, where the matter at the centre of a dispute is criminal, raising issues of criminal liability, section 69 of the Constitution provides that 'every person accused of an offence has the right to a fair and public trial within a reasonable time before an independent and impartial court. In addition, in the determination of civil rights and obligations, every person has a right to a fair, speedy and public hearing within a reasonable time before an independent and impartial court, tribunal or other forum established by law. Further, every person has the right of access to the courts, or to some other tribunal or forum established by law for the resolution of any dispute. And, every person has a right, at their own expense, to choose and be represented by a legal

130. *Chimango & Another v. International Committee of the Red Cross* HH 96/16; *Nduna v. Proton Bakeries* HH 164/15; *Muneka v. Manica Bus Company* 2013 (1) ZLR 81 (H).

131. A question of law involves the application or interpretation of the law or what the correct legal test is. The best definition of what a question of law is in Zimbabwe was laid down by Gubbay CJ in *Muzuwa v. United Bottlers (Pvt) Ltd* 1994 (1) ZLR 217 (S) in which he stated as follows: First, it means a question which the law itself has authoritatively answered to the exclusion of the right of the court to answer the question as it thinks fit in accordance with what is considered to be the truth and justice of the matter. Second, it means a question as to what the law is. Thus, an appeal on a question of law means an appeal in which the question for argument and determination is what the true rule of law is on a certain matter. And third, any question which is within the province of the judge instead of the jury is called a question of law. I respectively adopt this classification, although the third sense is of no relevance to a matter such as this.

132. Munyaradzi Gwisai, *Labour and Employment Law in Zimbabwe: Relations of Work under Neo-Colonial Capitalism* (2006).

133. Lovemore Madhuku, *Labour Law in Zimbabwe* (2015).

practitioner before any court, tribunal or forum'. It is also worth noting that the inclusion of sports matters in the Constitution means that there is also room for virtually any member of the public to sue a league or team that fails to deliver a satisfactory product after they have paid to watch an event. This is because several associations are established with the remit to afford entertainment to the public, and so, they charge members of the public to watch under the guise that competition is fair and not staged. If it should appear that this is not done honestly and is done to deprive the public of their money, then criminal and civil liability attaches. With respect to corruption, abuse of office, and match-fixing, the Criminal Law (Codification and Reform) Act prohibits corruption. Interestingly, some sports teams in Zimbabwe are sponsored and supported financially by local authorities that rely on public funds. And so, justice may demand in some instances that the public hold the authorities criminally or civilly liable.

99. Where all these avenues fail, or are inadequate, collective job action, organised at a central level by employee groupings, commonly called trade unions, or by employer groupings, has grown to be accepted as a key technique in resolving disputes effectively, efficiently, and expeditiously. Depending on whether it is employees or employers acting as a collective, such collective job action can consist of strikes by employees, lock-ins by employees against employers, sit-ins by employees who come to work but do not work, or, lockouts by employers to prevent employees from working.[134] In Zimbabwean employment law generally, section 65(2) and (3) of the Constitution provides that except for members of the security services, every person has the right to form and join trade unions and employee or employers' organisations of their choice, and to participate in the lawful activities of those unions and organisations and that every employee has the right to participate in collective job action, including the right to strike, sit in, withdraw their labour and to take other similar concerted action, but a law may restrict the exercise of this right in order to maintain essential services. In complement to this, section 104(1) of the Labour Act recognises that all employees, workers committees and trade unions have the right to resort to collective job action to resolve disputes of interest.

100. While the Act only distinguishes disputes of right and disputes of interest,[135] a dispute is collective if it involves a number of players collectively.[136] And section 105 recognises collective job action in the form of strike or lockout as techniques for resolving employment disputes where this is done lawfully in terms of section 104 of the Act. Because the same law applies to sports, it is clear then that Zimbabwean sports law recognises the right of any employees involved in sport to be involved in lawful collective job action. The same right is extended to employers who are allowed to act collectively and lock out employees, for example, provided that this is done lawfully.

134. Sections 104 and 105 of the Labour Act.
135. Tapiwa G Kasuso, *Labour Law Zimbabwe Open University Labour Law Module* (2019).
136. Kasuso, *supra* n. 35, at 3.

101. Aside from all this, redress, where disputes arise, can also be secured through administrative law. This is because the Constitution protects everyone's right to administrative justice which concerns how people interact as individuals when the government, or those working on its behalf, and even private entities, act in ways that appear wrong, unfair or unjust. It encompasses matters of everyday importance to all of us, such as housing, education, healthcare, immigration, planning, social security and taxation. In securing these rights, section 68 of the Constitution provides that every person has a right to administrative conduct that is lawful, prompt, efficient, reasonable, proportionate, impartial and both substantively and procedurally fair and that any person whose right, freedom, interest or legitimate expectation has been adversely affected by administrative conduct has the right to be given promptly and in writing the reasons for the conduct. These rights mean that anyone slighted in the above ways can proceed to court. Importantly, though, it is the principle of the Zimbabwean courts 'not to interfere with the internal matters of registered societies'. There are, however, exceptions to this principle, especially where the need to safeguard against any unconstitutional act is on the verge of being infringed. Zimbabwean courts have also intervened in the internal matters of sports associations in Zimbabwe by issuing injunctions and declarators where an association attempts to amend its statutes and to conduct elections in contravention with the procedural regularities set out in the statutes of the said association.[137] The supremacy of the national courts over sports tribunals was emphasised in *Highlanders Football Club v. Zimbabwe Football Association and Others*[138] where the court noted that it 'has inherent jurisdiction over all matters in Zimbabwe. The High Court further held that it had jurisdiction to issue an injunction restraining ZIFA from amending the player status of individuals without following due process'.

§3. The Welfare of Participants

102. There is a general constitutional obligation imposed on the state, in section 30 of the Constitution, to take all practical measures, within the limits of the resources available to it, to provide social security and social care to those who are in need. Insofar as Zimbabwean employment law is concerned generally, it is well recognised that protecting, or at least attempting to protect, the welfare of employees while they are employed and after their retirement from work is an important part of employment law. Unsurprisingly, this is a position that has been mirrored in sports employment law in Zimbabwe.

103. Indeed, drawing from several pieces of legislation that form part of the complement of employment laws in Zimbabwe, such as the Factories and Works

---

137. *Mukuhlani, supra* n. 2.
138. HB 424/2003.

Act,[139] Public Health Act,[140] and the Pneumoconiosis Act,[141] sports employment law in Zimbabwe requires employers to care for the welfare of employees while they are still employed by imposing a duty on them to ensure safe and healthy working conditions for employees. This includes, *inter alia*, providing proper training machinery and equipment, and adequately trained and competent supervisory staff. And in terms of the Labour Act, if employers fail to meet their health and safety obligations, the affected employees are not in breach of their contract if they withdraw their labour until the dangerous situation is corrected.[142] Worthy of separate mention here is the National Social Security Authority's (NSSA's) Statutory Instrument[143] which stems from the provision in section 3 of the NSSA Act.[144] The said section empowers the Minister through a notice in a statutory instrument to establish one or more schemes for the provision of benefits to, or in respect of, all employees or such classes of employees as may be specified in the notice and may in like manner amend or abolish any such schemes. Relying on this directive, the Minister enacted the NSSA (Accident Prevention and Workers' Compensation Scheme) Notice, 1990 (S.I. 68 of 1990) which creates a scheme that covers compensation for work-related injuries, deaths and diseases in the workplace. The statutory instrument, in section 8, abolishes any common law claims for damages which an employee may have and states that any employee or dependant to whom the scheme applies is not permitted to resort to the common law for compensation for work-related injuries, death or diseases. The prohibition is a quid pro quo for compelling the employer to make contributions to the Workers' Compensation Fund. It is only fair that employers be protected from common law actions. The overall purpose of such a state of affairs is to promote the public interest in having an orderly, guaranteed and no-fault-based compensation scheme for work-related injuries, deaths and diseases.

104. The compensatory framework under the scheme has three obvious advantages not available under the common law. First, it is a no-fault scheme. The employee is not required to prove any fault on the part of the employer. All that is required is to prove injury, death or disease arising out of and in the course of employment. Second, in an action under the common law, there is always the risk of the employer being financially unable to pay the damages claimed. This risk is removed under the scheme as payment is from the insurance fund. Third, the scheme grants some benefits not available under the common law, such as to the dependants of employees killed as a result of a work-related accident or disease.

---

139. Chapter 14:08. This Act provides for the registration and control of factories, the regulation of conditions of work in factories, supervision of the use of machinery and precautions against accidental injury to persons employed on structural work.
140. Chapter 15:09. This Act creates the legal framework for the protection of public health in Zimbabwe. For this purpose, it provides for powers of the administration to regulate and control slaughter of animals, food production and handling, food and water supply, animal diseases, etc.
141. Chapter 15:08. It seeks to protect those working in dusty occupations from the danger of contracting pneumoconiosis.
142. Section 104(4) of the Labour Act.
143. National Social Security Authority (Accident Prevention and Workers' Compensation Scheme) Notice, 1990 (S.I. 68 of 1990).
144. Chapter 17:04.

And, because of its merits, this is a position that has repeatedly been affirmed by the courts,[145] and it is a scheme that applies to several employees in sports. As such, employees' common law claims in sports where they fall within the scope of the scheme established by the statutory instrument have fallen away.

105. Quite separate to this, and drawing from the section 30 constitutional obligation on the state to take all practical measures, within the limits of the resources available to it, to provide social security and social care to those who are in need, sports employment law in Zimbabwe looks to protect the welfare of employees after retirement through the provision for compulsory Pensions and Other Benefits Scheme created by NSSA which has been established through the NSSA (Pensions and Other Benefits Scheme).[146]

106. Notably, while the Scheme has been regarded as imposing a 'tax',[147] it only applies to employees who, together with their employers, pay compulsory monthly contributions to the Scheme with the employer obligated to deduct the employee's contributions from the earnings payable to the employee and pay them, together with the employer's own contributions, to the fund. Of note, any person who has ceased to be an employee but had contributed for at least twelve months may continue to pay his or her contributions to the fund as a 'voluntary contributor' provided he or she is under the age of 60.

107. It is also important to note that participants in sports are at liberty to join private schemes which are regulated by law through the Pension and Provident Funds Act.[148] In terms of this Act, no person may establish a pension fund unless it

145. *See Workers' Compensation Commissioner v. FA Stewart (Pvt) Ltd* 1990 (2) ZLR 376 and *Sibanda v. Independence Gold Mining Zimbabwe (Pvt) Ltd & Another* 2003 (2) ZLR 155 (H). Also *see Ncube v. Wankie Colliery Co Another* 2007 (1) ZLR 96 (H) where it was held that 'the plaintiffs cause of action had been abolished by the NSSA scheme. The common law action is not permissible. There is no liability for pain and suffering under the NSSA scheme. It was held further that the junior employee who caused the accident was not in management and therefore fell outside section 9 of SI 68/1990. SI 68/1990 is a social insurance scheme. This is because "the employer is obliged to make contributions to the Workers' Compensation Fund". Under the common law, it is the duty of the employer to provide safe working conditions. Workers do not make contributions to the Fund'.

146. Notice, 1993 (S1 393/1993).

147. In *Nyambirai v. NSSA and Anor* 1995 (2) ZLR 1 (S), the State Pension Scheme faced a severe test. The first question for the court was to determine whether or not the contributions were a form of 'tax'. The court identified four essential requirements of a tax as follows: (i) it is a compulsory and not an optional contribution, (ii) it is imposed by the Legislature or other competent public authority, (iii) it is imposed upon the public as a whole or a substantial sector thereof and (iv) the revenue from it is to be utilised for the public benefit and to provide a service in the public interest. The applicant argued that the fourth requirement was lacking, since the benefits under the scheme only applied to members or their survivors. There was no direct benefit to members of the public in general. The court disagreed. It considered the social and economic policies which moved the Government to introduce a compulsory pension scheme and concluded that it was for the public benefit and was a service in the public interest. The main policy was to provide national social protection and this was manifestly in the public interest. The conclusion was therefore that the contributions were a 'tax'.

148. Chapter 24:09.

is registered or provisionally registered. Once registered completely, a fund becomes a body corporate capable of suing and being sued in its corporate name and shall have assets, rights, liabilities and obligations pertaining to its business. Further, each fund shall have rules which must comply with such requirements as may be prescribed from time to time, and presently, the rules in force are contained in the Pension and Provident Funds Regulations of 1991.[149] These regulations provide, *inter alia*, that every employee on the full-time permanent staff of an employer who is below the age of 55 years has an automatic right to join a fund established for or covering employees of his or her employer. Separately, the regulations provide that once an employee has joined a pension fund, he or she shall not be permitted to withdraw from membership as long as he or she is still an employee of a participating employer except if he or she becomes a member of another registered fund established for the benefit of employees of the same employer. Lastly, the regulations provide that the minimum retirement age is 55 years and the maximum is 70 years.

149. SI 323/1991.

Part III. Doping and Sport

Chapter 1. General Issues

108. Doping refers to the use of banned athletic performance-enhancing drugs by participants in sport either of their own volition or, as has often occurred, as part of well-structured and coordinated state regimes.[150] The reasons for the ban range from concern over the health risks of performance-enhancing drugs, the equality of opportunity for athletes, to the exemplary effect of drug-free sport for the public. And because doping is universally regarded as unethical and contrary to the ethos of sports of guaranteeing every team or athlete a fair chance of winning and protecting athletes' health, regulating its occurrence has become a massive concern at all levels of sport across the world.

109. At the international level, WA has been at the forefront of fighting doping in sports. It has adopted Rules and Regulations to ensure that athletes do not engage in doping, and those who flout these rules and regulations are severely punished. In these efforts, WA has been joined by the IOC which works with other international agencies to ensure that all events organised under their auspices are doping-free. Perhaps the most notable Agency in this regard is WADA which was established on 10 November 1999 in Lausanne to promote and coordinate the fight against doping in sports internationally. The Agency was set up as a foundation under the initiative of the IOC with the support and participation of intergovernmental organisations, governments, public authorities, and other public and private bodies fighting doping in sports and consists of equal representatives from the Olympic Movement and public authorities. All the international federations and Member States under the IOC are supposed to be signed on to the WADA Code which ensures that both athletes and teams are susceptible to various sanctions under the WADA Code, such as suspensions, disqualification of results and allocation of forfeited prize money thus ensuring that the phenomenon of doping in sports is combated and sportsmen and women compete fairly. In addition, WADA expects member countries to establish National Anti-doping Organizations (NADOs) which will spearhead the implementation of the code.

150. UNESCO, *What Is Doping?*, http://www.unesco.org/new/en/social-and-human-sciences/themes/anti-doping/youth-space/what-is-doping/ (accessed 30 Nov. 2019).

110. Zimbabwe, by virtue of being a member of all these institutions with their subsidiaries such as NAAZ and the ZOC already established, has committed to taking positive steps to fight doping in sports. In addition to this, Zimbabwe has been a signatory to the United Nations Educational, Scientific and Cultural Organization (UNESCO) International Convention against Doping in Sport since December 2011. By doing so, Zimbabwe reasserted its commitment to WADA's World Anti-Doping Code and assented to the Convention's zero-tolerance spirit against doping by undertaking to: restrict the availability of prohibited substances or methods to athletes (except for legitimate medical purposes), including measures against trafficking; facilitate doping controls and support national testing programmes; withhold financial support from athletes and athlete support personnel who commit an anti-doping rule violation, or from sporting organisations that are not in compliance with the WADA Code; encourage producers and distributors of nutritional supplements to establish 'best practice' in the labelling, marketing and distribution of products which might contain prohibited substances; and support the provision of anti-doping education to athletes and the wider sporting community.[151]

151. UNESCO, *supra* n. 150.

Chapter 2. Public Regulation

111. Consistent with sentiments expressed in the Constitution of Zimbabwe which are against corruption and promote fairness, justice, equality, and equal opportunity, there is a great public interest in stopping doping in Zimbabwean sport. In 2014, UNESCO gave a USD 19,000 grant to the Ministry of Sports to enable the Ministry to undertake anti-doping education and awareness activities.[152]

112. However, such public interest in stopping doping has not translated to a public regulation framework tackling doping in Zimbabwe sports. There is no dedicated legislation on doping in sports. However, there is some relevant drug control legislation which criminalises possession and trade in certain drugs associated with doping, such as performance-enhancing drugs, testosterone, and human growth hormone. Such legislation is, therefore, a useful source of sports law in Zimbabwe.[153]

113. Importantly, though, the reality in Zimbabwean sport is that there really is not enough money to get the authorities to establish a pronounced public anti-doping regulatory framework. For instance, athletics has been rocked by doping allegations amid fears the country's sporting fraternity could be enveloped by this scandal due to the unavailability of a WADA accredited laboratory locally.[154] The situation got worse following the closure of the only laboratory on the continent that was located in South Africa.

---

152. ZOC, *Anti-doping in Sport Takes Centre Stage*, http://zoc.co.zw/anti-doping-in-sport-takes-centre-stage/ (accessed 20 Mar. 2020).
153. The relevant legislation includes: Dangerous Drugs (Amendment) Regulations, 2019, Statutory Instrument 232 of 2019; Medicines and Allied Substances Control (Complementary Medicines) (Amendment) Regulations 2018 (No. 1); Dangerous Drugs (Production of Cannabis for Medicinal and Scientific Use) Regulations, SI 62 of 2018; Medicines and Allied Substances Control (General) (Amendment) Regulations, 2016 (No. 29), SI 99 of 2016; Dangerous Drugs Regulations RGN 1111 of 1975; Dangerous Drugs Amendment Regulations SI 33 of 2015; Medicines and Allied Substances Control (Homeopathic Remedies) (Repeal) Regulations, 2015, SI 96 of 2015; Medicines and Allied Substances Control (Complementary Medicines) Regulations, 2015, SI 97 of 2015; Medicines and Allied Substances Control General Regulations 1991 SI 150 of 1991. *See also* the National Medicines Policy of Zimbabwe of 2011.
154. Sikhumbuzo Moyo, *Doping Claims Rock Zimbabwe Athletics*, https://www.chronicle.co.zw/doping-claims-rock-zimbabwe-athletics/ (accessed 18 Nov. 2019).

Chapter 3. Private Regulation

114. Deficiencies in the public regulation framework have left private regulation as the most prominent form of doping. This is most prominently done through the common law where it is applicable. For instance, where participation in events is based on contractual relationships, where competitors are required by contract not to cheat, if they do so, they will be in breach of contract. This creates a cause of action against the offending party. Alternatively, the private regulation of doping can be achieved through the common law of delict which deals with 'the circumstances in which one person can claim compensation from another for harm that has been suffered'.[155] For instance, when one competitor enhances performance illegally and wins an event or secures some benefit from this, that person can reasonably be sued for unjustified enrichment. There is also the possibility of a suit for damages where anyone harmed by the deceitful act can successfully establish that harm was suffered due to the offending act.

115. Quite aside from private legal regulation through the common law, the regulation of doping is also done privately by non-governmental institutions involved in sports governance. To this end, it is interesting to note that the most comprehensive anti-doping programme in Zimbabwe is carried out by the ZOC in partnership with WADA. In theory, testing in Zimbabwe is random, but can also be targeted, and can take place both in and out of competition – this means it can be after a game, at training or even at your own home. Banned substances are split into two categories, performance-enhancing drugs, such as steroids and supplements, and recreational drugs, such as cocaine, ecstasy, and cannabis. It is worth noting that the WADA Code and the authorities treat recreational drugs in the same manner as performance-enhancing; therefore, the process and suspensions are the same. Strict Liability rules apply and players are fully responsible for any banned substances found in their system regardless of how they got there. Some of the offences are the presence of a banned substance in a sample, refusal to provide a sample, abusive or insulting words or behaviour towards a Doping Control official, interfering with the drug testing process. All banned substances are outlined on the prohibited list, which is regularly updated. The latest prohibited list can be found on the WADA website.[156] In addition to this, the Zimbabwean Institute for Drug Free Sport (ZIDS), an affiliate of the South African Institute for Drug-Free Sport (SAIDS), has emerged as an institution that has looked to establish uncodified anti-doping rules which are borrowed from different jurisdictions and the WADA Code.[157]

155. Loubser, *supra* n. 37.
156. FUZ, *Anti-doping*, http://www.fuz.co.zw/playerservices.php?id=8 (accessed 20 Mar. 2020).
157. South African Institute for Drug-Free Sport, *Anti-doping Rules 2019*, https://www.drugfreesport.org.za/wp-content/uploads/2019/04/SAIDS-Anti-Doping-Rules-2019.pdf (accessed 20 Mar. 2020).

116. It is difficult to establish whether this manner of private regulation has made some headway. Relevant institutions have either not exhibited the necessary commitment to anti-doping or have failed to test athletes effectively due to resource constraints with the result that doping may be going unchecked. However, it is not all doom and gloom. There are some successes that have been recorded in the anti-doping effort. Perhaps the most celebrated was in 2014 when Devon Chafa tested positive for a glucocorticosteroid called prednisone after playing in the Zimbabwean Men National Football Team's 4-2 loss against Egypt in Harare. This led to him receiving a six-month ban from playing football in sanctioned matches.[158] Significantly, though, such successes are too few and far between. The reality is that there are deficiencies in the anti-doping regime which mean that the most important regulator insofar as doping is concerned is the athlete who has hopes of competing in international competitions where testing is prevalent. For this reason, it has become very important for athletes to be educated on doping, something which the Zimbabwe Olympians Association President Abel Chimukoko and ZOC Secretary General Anna Mguni have identified as an exceedingly important quality for athletes to have.[159]

158. Newsday, *PSL to Sniff for Drugs*, https://www.newsday.co.zw/2019/03/psl-to-sniff-for-drugs/ (accessed 20 Mar. 2020).

159. World Olympians Association, *Zimbabwe Olympians Unite to Tackle Doping in Sport*, https://olympians.org/news/481/zimbabwe-olympians-unite-to-tackle-doping-in-sport/ (accessed 20 Mar. 2020).

Part IV. Sport and Commerce

Chapter 1. General Issues

117. Sports generate an inordinate amount of revenue. However, while public policy dictates that participants who are actively involved in the generation of revenue should benefit, it is difficult to always honour public policy for several reasons. For instance, it is not always possible to calculate how much revenue is generated when the event is on. It is also possible to generate revenues well after the event and it is not always easy to know that revenues are generated. Some revenues, such as proceeds of gambling, may be obtained unlawfully. On a similar note, revenues may be generated even without staging an event as is the case where sponsorship revenue is generated or where revenues are generated through such activities as merchandising. Separately, it is not always the case that participants control how revenue is generated when an event is on. And so, participants will not always be able to benefit. It is in the public interest that participants benefit. If they do not, they will look for ways to benefit. It also makes sense that an owner who pays for a club and invests in it should do what they want, but such freedom may be against public policy. Experience shows that it is in the public interest that those participating in sport should benefit as much as possible; otherwise, they will look to benefit in unscrupulous ways.[160]

118. And so, any viable body of sports law should put in place a public regulation framework that ensures that participants draw the possible benefit at all times

160. For instance, Asiagate-concerns first came to light in Zimbabwe when the football association (ZIFA) revealed in February 2011 that there was an investigation taking place into tours in which the national team had taken part in between 2007 and 2009. Players involved in those tours subsequently admitted to throwing matches for money. The probe revealed that not only had Asian gaming syndicates paid each player in the Zimbabwe squad EUR 2,500–EUR 3,500 in cash for each match lost, but also that last July, Monomotapa Football Club had twice impersonated the country's national team and played in Malaysia in international friendlies. As planned, they lost 4-0 and were handsomely rewarded. It has since been announced that eighty Zimbabwean footballers have been suspended by ZIFA pending the outcome of hearings in front of an independent ethics committee, which has been established as a direct consequence of the revelations. The international friendlies are thought to have been arranged specifically for the purposes of betting. Considering the sheer number of people who were willing to compromise moral codes that are particularly celebrated in sport such as not cheating to, this points to a level of dissatisfaction with economic rewards for sporting excellence.

from their efforts. In addition to this, any viable body of sports law should put in place a private regulation framework which empowers participants to accord the participants intellectual property rights so that they can regulate privately and benefit from their rights.

Chapter 2. Public Regulation

119. Zimbabwean law encourages entrepreneurship. Indeed, section 13(1) of Zimbabwe's Constitution provides, *inter alia*, that the state and all institutions and agencies of government at every level must endeavour to facilitate rapid and equitable development, and in particular, must take measures to promote private initiative and self-reliance; foster agricultural, commercial, industrial, technological and scientific development; and foster the development of industrial and commercial enterprises in order to empower Zimbabwean citizens. However, the public policy informed by the preamble to the same Constitution demands that people should benefit from their efforts, skill, talent, and ingenuity. Therefore, beyond ensuring that employees are given remuneration for services rendered, Zimbabwean sports law looks to ensure that participants receive portions of the revenues generated from their efforts, skill, talent, and ingenuity, in several ways. Some of the most notable ways in which this is done, which are discussed below, include, by ensuring that participants benefit from the sale of media rights and from any sponsorship and merchandising revenue that is generated. The law regulates each of these scenarios in different ways and so each is deserving of a separate discussion.

§1. Media and Television Rights

120. Improvements in technology mean that one no longer needs to attend sporting events in person. The events can now be broadcast across different media to wherever the consumer of the product is. This has several commercial implications for sports. For instance, it means that participants can showcase their skill and talent to larger audiences, thereby creating a wider fan base that they can sell their products to and generate revenues that ultimately affect their remuneration. Broadcasts are also a revenue-generating tool for participants because they attract a greater audience which advertisers will be drawn to and will look to advertise their products during the broadcast and they are quite willing to pay handsomely for the privilege. However, broadcasts are usually run by non-participants, and so, there is a need for revenues to be shared in reasonably fair ways. There is also the need to determine such issues as who holds the rights to the product being broadcast. In more recent times, the issue of illegal broadcasting has become particularly problematic. There are also questions surrounding unsanctioned broadcasts, using a mobile phone, for example. Importantly, all these are issues that the Zimbabwean sports law looks to regulate.

121. To this end, broadcasting sporting events is covered in terms of the law. The main pieces of legislation include the Zimbabwe Broadcasting (Commercialisation) Act 26 of 2001 and the Copyright and Neighbouring Rights [Chapter 26:05]. The predecessor of the Zimbabwe Broadcasting (Commercialisation) Act is the Zimbabwe Broadcasting Act [Chapter 12:01]. The latter had, in its section 3, established the Zimbabwe Broadcasting Corporation (ZBC). It is wholly owned and controlled by the state. The ZBC was not repealed but was dismantled as a statutory corporation and its functions were conferred on successor companies which were registered under the Companies Act [Chapter 24:03]. In terms of section 61 of the Constitution, state-owned broadcasters should be impartial and should afford fair opportunity for the presentation of divergent views and dissenting opinion.[161] This has allowed participants to showcase their skill and talent to larger audiences, thereby creating a wider fan base that they can sell their products to and generate revenues that ultimately affect their remuneration. At the same time, intellectual property laws allow the participants to retain the rights to the product remain with the participants. The PSL Rules, for example, provide that television and radio rights for all matches of the League shall belong to the League and no matches may be televised or filmed without the consent of the League. Separately, in cricket, matches are broadcast across the world and broadcast revenues generated go to the ICC which then shares them with ZC. And so, the law effectively ensures that participants benefit from revenues generated through broadcasting their events.

122. Separately, advertising during broadcasts is also regulated by law. However, advertising revenues go to the broadcaster. And it must be accounted for that the broadcaster bears the costs of broadcasting, and so, public policy also recognises that the broadcaster should benefit from any revenues generated due to the broadcast. And so, insofar as advertising is concerned, it is often the estimation of these revenues that will be relied on to fix sums that the broadcaster must pay participants in order to get permission to broadcast. And so, in this way, the law ensures that broadcasters and participants benefit from revenues generated through advertising.

123. By the same token, the sports law also recognises the status of advertisers. In addition, the law rewards advertisers by allowing them to benefit from their ingenuity and ability to attract consumers through their adverts. To this end, adversely impacting adverts or passing off another's advert as one's own is criminalised.

124. Copyright law protects the rights in broadcasts. In Zimbabwe, copyright is governed by the Copyright and Neighbouring Rights Act [Chapter 26:05]. Section 9 thereof defines copyright as a real right which subsists in work in terms of the Act and gives the owner of copyright exclusive rights in dealing with the copyright. For copyright to subsist, there should be an original work which is fixed. The requirement for fixation does not apply to broadcasts and programme-carrying signals. Works which are eligible for copyright protection include literary works, artistic works, audio-visual works, sounding recordings, programme-carrying signals and published editions. In terms of section 10(3) of the Act, a broadcast shall not be eligible for copyright protection until it has been broadcasted. Similarly, a programme-carrying signal is only eligible for protection after it has been transmitted.

125. Section 21 of the Act provides that copyright in a broadcast vests in the owner who has exclusive rights to do or authorise reproduction of the broadcast

161. *Firinne Trust and Others v. Zimbabwe Broadcasting Corporation* HMA-23-19.

directly or indirectly, including making of a still photograph from it, rebroadcasting of the broadcast, making the broadcasting available on a public computer network, and causing the broadcast to be transmitted in a cable programme services. However, there are exceptions to these exclusive rights which allow the recording of programmes and broadcasts for purposes of subsequent viewing or listening.[162] Thus, where a programme is recorded for the sole purpose of enabling it to be viewed or listened to at a more convenient time, there is no breach of copyright. Such a recording should only be used for the purpose for which it was made and should not be distributed to any person outside the family of the person who made it. Furthermore, it should not be performed in public.

126. In the context of sports law, sports associations and their members are the owners of copyright, including broadcasting rights. For instance, Article 71 of the Statutes of the ZIFA provides that ZIFA and its members are the original owners of the rights emanating from competitions and other events under its jurisdiction. These include reproduction and broadcasting rights. A similar provision is found under Article 64 of the Premier Soccer League (PSL) Statutes. Furthermore, Order 28.5 of the PSL Rules and Regulations explicitly states that television and radio rights for all matches of the League shall belong to the League and no matches may be televised or filmed without the consent of the League. Currently, the PSL has an agreement with the ZBC for the broadcasting of matches. This agreement comes after the expiry of the one the PSL had with Multichoice.

127. There are various statutory remedies for the breach of copyright which are provided for in section 52 of the Act. These include damages,[163] interdict,[164] attachment, rendering of account, delivery up of infringing copies or articles used in the infringement of copyright. In addition, there are criminal sanctions for copyright infringement. Section 59(3) thereof criminalises broadcasting or rebroadcasting, or transmitting in a cable service, knowing that copyright subsists in the signal and that the rebroadcast constitutes an infringement of the copyright. Such an infringement attracts a fine not exceeding level ten or an imprisonment term not exceeding two years or both.[165]

§2. SPONSORSHIP

128. Sponsorship arrangements typically arise when anyone who is in business or who has some other motivation, looking to improve his/her own standing and perceptions among the public, will look to associate with the participants and the teams they play for in order to benefit commercially from the goodwill generated by the participants and teams they play for. This can be done in several ways,

162. Section 41 of the Copyright and Neigbouring Rights Act [Chapter 26:05].
163. *Grama Records (Private) Ltd and Others v. Chimusoro* HH-22-07.
164. *The Trustees of Mukono Family and Mukonotricks (Pvt) Ltd Karpeg Investment (Pvt) Ltd and Others* HH-30-08; *Livera Trading (Pvt) Ltd and Others v. Tornbridge Assets Ltd and Others* CCZ-13-2016.
165. *State v. Moyo and Tshaba* HH-28-04.

including: agreements whereby one party agrees to make payment to another in consideration for being given publicity in connection with an event or events staged by the second party; agreements whereby a party pays a certain amount to or towards certain expenses of a public figure, sporting figures or team in consideration for endorsement by that public figure, sporting figure or team of certain products or services sold or provided by the first party; agreements whereby one party, either for free or for consideration, provides certain playing or other equipment, products, supplies or services for use by an individual, team or entity in consideration for endorsement by the individual, team or entity of the sponsor's product, supplies and/or services (as the case may be). Such endorsement could take the form of brand association, advertising and/or promotional opportunities. Examples of this type of sponsorship agreement include an official sports drinks sponsor, a clothing sponsor or an official airline sponsor. In addition, a sponsor could be categorised as: a team sponsor who sponsors a team for either a fixed period, for example, a season, or for an indefinite period, or, for a particular match, event, competition or tournament; an event sponsor who sponsors an entire event and depending on different variables, such sponsor could even acquire the naming rights for the event and possibly, future events; an individual sponsor who sponsor an individual sportsperson, in which case the sponsor is often referred to as an 'endorsement sponsor'.

129. Probably because sponsorship is proving difficult to generate in Zimbabwe, the statutory law on sponsorship is not all that developed. The most notable legislative provision that provides for sponsorship is the ITA which exempts sponsors from paying taxes, reflects the drive to encourage the growth of sponsorship.[166] And so, sponsorship is predominantly regulated based on the common law of contract. And so, the common law of contract regulates sponsorship quite extensively. Effectively, a sponsor must make terms clear. The person accepting must deliver what is promised. And in all that, participants have a legitimate expectation that they will benefit from sponsorship revenue. If they should not benefit, then it would be sufficient grounds for an unjustified enrichment claim. Alternatively, they could alert the sponsor to the breach of contract. Similarly, a sponsor who benefits from affiliation with participants but fails to deliver the quid pro quo can also be sued for unjustified enrichment.[167] It is also worth noting that sponsorship can generate the sort of revenue for teams and clubs that can impact matters that matter to the public, such as gate fees. Because the Constitution advocates non-corruption, this means members of the public can sue for mismanagement or corruption.

§3. MERCHANDISING

130. As sports have become bigger and transcended national boundaries, merchandising, a reference to the commercial exploitation of the name, badge, logo, or other trademark associated with a particular sporting property such as a team, individual, league, or event, in order to sell goods or services, has become a prominent

166. Chapter 23:06.
167. Mullin, Hardy & Sutton, *supra* n. 81.

practice. Common sporting merchandise includes replica shirts, team scarves, and other clothing and items bearing individual or team logos and images. The concern here has always been that when someone looks to benefit from merchandising, the participants in sport whose talent, skill, and efforts lead to merchandise having value should be adequately remunerated. And to secure consistency with public policy, rights owners often make money by entering into a contract with specialist manufacturers to produce the merchandising in return for payment. Ownership of the rights and the associated intellectual property remains with the person granting the licence, but the licensee is granted the right to use the intellectual property rights for the duration of and subject to the terms of the licence. The payment terms commonly involve an initial fee plus a royalty based on either units sold or revenue generated by sales of the merchandising. Interestingly, merchandising companies also benefit from sales revenues and often have rights to include their own logo on the merchandise.

131. Across this whole relationship, the Zimbabwean sports law plays three prominent roles. First, the law grants intellectual property rights to participants whose talent, skill, and efforts lead to merchandise having value. These rights allow these participants to benefit from revenues generated from the sale of such merchandise. In addition, and consistent with section 13(1) of Zimbabwe's Constitution, these rights are a measure taken by the state to promote private initiative and self-reliance. The rights also foster commercial, industrial, technological and scientific development and the development of industrial and commercial enterprises in order to empower Zimbabwean citizens. Second, the law criminalises the act of unlawfully benefitting from merchandising without a licence. This is a public interest matter because when participants do not benefit from the revenues generated from the exploitation of their talent, skill, and efforts, there is the possibility that this leads to actions that are contrary to the public interest, such as cheating in sports. Third, and also in the public interest, the law criminalises the counterfeiting of merchandise.

I. Law of Trademarks

132. Trademarks are at the heart of sports branding and merchandising. They are valuable assets and they bulked trust, confidence and loyalty in a product.[168] In Zimbabwe, trademarks are governed by the Trade Marks Act [Chapter 26:04]. Trademark is defined in section 2 of the Act as:

> '*trade mark*' means a mark which is used or proposed to be used in relation to goods or services for the purpose of –

168. Frank I. Schechter, *The Rational Basis of Trade Mark Protection*, 40 Harv. L. R. 813 (1927).

(a) indicating a connection in the course of trade between the goods or services and some person having the right, either as proprietor or as registered user, to use the mark, whether with or without any indication of the identity of that person; and
(b) distinguishing the goods or services in relation to which the mark is used or proposed to be used, from the same kind of goods or services connected in the course of trade with any other person.

133. In turn, a mark includes a distinguishing guise, slogan, device, brand, heading, label, ticket, name, signature, word, letter or numeral or any combination thereof, whether rendered in two-dimensional or three-dimensional form.[169]

134. Once a trademark is registered, it gives the registered owner of the trademark an exclusive right to use it in connection which the goods or services for which it is registered. Thus, the essence of trademark registration is that no other party should use the trademark.[170] Sports associations are the owners of trademarks. For instance, Article 72 of ZIFA Statutes provides that ZIFA and its members are exclusively responsible for authorising the distribution of image and sound and other data carriers of football matches and events within their jurisdiction.

135. The Act provides for remedies for infringements of this Act and these include the following:

(1) Civil remedies:[171]
 - Damages.[172]
 - Interdict.[173]
 - Attachment.[174]
 - Rendering of account.[175]
 - Delivery of improperly marked goods.[176]
(2) Anton Pillar Orders.[177]
(3) Criminal Penalties.[178]

169. *Zimbabwe Gelatine (Pvt) Ltd v. Cairns Food (Pvt) Ltd* SC-130-2002.
170. Section 8 of the Act. *CAPS United Football Club (Pty) Ltd v. CAPS Holdings Ltd and Another* SC-18-2008.
171. Section 9A of the Act.
172. Section 9A and 9C of the Act.
173. Section 9A of the Act. *Unilever P.L.C and Unilever South East Africa (Pvt) v. VIMCO (Pvt) Ltd and Registrar of Companies* HH-175-04.
174. Section 9A of the Act.
175. *Ibid.*
176. *Ibid.*
177. Section 9D of the Act.
178. Sections 92–96 of the Act.

II. Unlawful Competition

136. In addition to the protection of marks under the Trade Marks Act, there is also common law which caters for unregistered marks. Section 6 of the Trade Marks Act explicitly provides that the Act only applies to registered trademarks while common law applies to unregistered marks. It states that:

> No person shall be entitled to institute any proceedings to prevent, or to recover damages for, the infringement of an unregistered trade mark:
>
> Provided that nothing in this Act shall affect the right of any person, at common law, to bring an action against any other person for passing off goods or services as the goods or services of another person.

137. There are three actions under common law, namely: the general action of unlawful competition; passing off and injurious falsehood. Each of these will be explained below.

A. *The General Action of Unlawful Competition*

138. Unlawful competition is a blanket term that encompasses all the ways in which competition can be said to be unfair. The forms of unlawful competition include: passing off, misappropriating the advertising value of trademarks, piracy of a competitor's performance, comparative advertising, and misrepresentation of one's own performance, among others. It is well established that our common law recognises every person's right to carry on his trade without wrongful interference from others, including competitors. The right to protection from the unlawful competition requires a wrongful interference with another's rights as a trader. The rights in question are the right to goodwill, custom and business reputation. Therefore, competition in trade is in itself not unlawful; it is unlawful if it unreasonably infringes on the goodwill of a competitor. As a general rule, every person is entitled freely to carry on his trade or business in competition with his rivals. However, competition is essential for the operation of an efficient free-market economy as is the right to freedom of trade. Nonetheless, it is limited by the common law principle of unlawful competition as a form of delict under the Aquilian action.[179]

139. Generally, in order to succeed in an action based on unfair competition, the plaintiff must establish all the requisites of Aquilian liability, including proof that the defendant has committed a wrongful act. In such a case, the unlawfulness which is a requisite of Aquilian liability may fall into a category of clearly recognised illegality, namely trading in contravention of an express statutory prohibition; the making of fraudulent misrepresentations by the rival trader as to his own business; the passing off by a rival trader of his goods or business as being that of his competitor;

179. *Bress Designs (Pty) Ltd v. C Y Lounge Suite Manufacturers (Pty) Ltd & Another* 1991 (2) SA 455.

the publication by the rival trader of injurious falsehoods concerning his competitor's business; and the employment of physical assaults and intimidation designed to prevent a competitor from pursuing his trade.

140. Consequently, a competitor who has suffered patrimonial loss as a result of acts recognised as unlawful competition may institute the Aquilian action under the law of Delict in order to be compensated for this loss.

141. The business that has suffered at the hands of unlawful competition would then have to establish the following elements of delictual liability in order to succeed in the action: conduct; wrongfulness; fault; causation and harm.

142. The business instituting the action would have to prove that there was conduct on the part of the offending business. This conduct can be in the form of a commission or an omission, the former being positive physical acts and statements, while the latter is failure to do or say.

143. In addressing the issue of wrongfulness, there are two enquiries; first, has there been an infringement of a legally recognised interest/right? If the answer is in the affirmative, the second is, whether such infringement occurred in a legally reprehensible or unreasonable manner? The question then is: when is the infringement of goodwill of a competitor wrong? In *Geary and Son (Pty) Ltd v. Gove*,[180] emphasis was placed upon criteria such as fairness and honesty in competition and it was said:

> Fairness and honesty are themselves somewhat vague and elastic terms but, while they may not provide a scientific or indeed infallible guide in all cases to the limits of lawful competition, they are relevant criteria which have been used in the past and which, in my view, may be used in the future in the development of the law relating to competition in trade.

144. In addition, in judging fairness and honesty, regard is had to *boni mores* and to the general sense of justice of the community. The court in *Atlas Organic Fertilizers (Pty) Ltd v. Pikkewyn Ghwano (Pty) Ltd and Others*[181] stated that:

> While fairness and honesty are relevant criteria in deciding whether competition is unfair, they are not the only criteria. Questions of public policy may be important in a particular case, e.g the importance of a free market and of competition in our economic system. Public Policy is the general sense of justice in the community, the *boni mores* manifested in public opinion. In determining and applying this norm in a particular case, the interests of the competing parties have to be weighed, bearing in mind also the interests of society. As this

---

180. 1964 (1) SA 434 (A) at 441.
181. 1981 (2) SA 173 (T).

norm cannot exist *in vacuo*, the morals of the market place, the business ethics of that section of the community where the norm is to be applied, are of major importance in its determination.

145. The element on fault focuses on the legal blameworthiness of the defendant. The defendant's fault can be in the form of either intent (*dolus*) or negligence (culpa). Instituting an Aquilian action requires the plaintiff to establish negligence or economic loss.

146. There should be a causal connection between the harm suffered by the plaintiff and the infringing conduct of the defendant. Causation involves two enquiries: first, whether there is a factual link between the defendant's conduct and the harm suffered by the plaintiff (factual causation). If in the affirmative, second, to what extent should the defendant be legally responsible for the consequences induced by his conduct (legal causation). Causation aims at ensuring that the defendant is held liable only for those consequences that are strongly linked to his conduct.

147. The law of delict presupposes an entitlement to damages for the harm inflicted. The damages under delict can be either patrimonial or non-patrimonial. In the case of infringement of the plaintiff's goodwill, the plaintiff seeks, among other things, damages for patrimonial loss. This is a calculable pecuniary loss or a reduction in the plaintiff's estate resulting from the defendant's wrongful conduct. Therefore, once the plaintiff can establish that they have suffered harm then they are entitled to damages.

148. An important case on unlawful competition relating to broadcasting is that of *eBotswana (Pty) Ltd v. Sentech (Pty) Ltd and Others.*[182] This is a case that discussed the general action of unlawful competition. The facts of the case were that eBotswana, a private television channel operating in Botswana, brought an application by way of motion proceedings to prevent private viewing of South African Broadcasting Corporation (SABC) channels. The motion proceedings were based on a delictual action under the Aquilian action. The SABC operated the South African channels of SABC 1, SABC 2 and SABC 3, which were transmitted from Sentech (Pty) Ltd's satellite. The signals from these channels were spilling over into the Botswana territory, and people in Botswana were able to view them freely, through decoders which were programmed to decrypt the signal. This greatly affected eBotswana's revenue streams. The applicants stated that they rely on advertisements in order to generate revenue, the SABC channels deprived eBotswana of its viewers and, as a result, persons willing to advertise on the television station.

149. eBotswana stated that Sentech was in unlawful competition with it because Sentech was not licensed to broadcast channels in Botswana, and so, by its omission of not securing the signals, they were infringing on eBotswana's goodwill and right to attract customers in the form of advertisers. It was stated in the court that

182. 2013 (6) SA 327 (GSJ).

the applicant must satisfy the court, even in motion proceedings based on the Acquilian action, that it has a clear right to both the declaratory and mandatory orders sought, as well a clear right to an order entitling it to hold an enquiry into damages. The pertinent issue in the case was whether or not the actions of Sentech were wrongful. In determining this, the court considered whether Sentech owed eBotswana a duty of care, by applying the *boni mores* criterion. It was held that Sentech did owe eBotswana a duty of care and that failure by Sentech to secure the signals was wrongfulness on its part. By its actions, or lack thereof, to secure the signals, Sentech infringed on the right to goodwill of eBotswana, unlawfully competing with it where Sentech was not licensed, and causing eBotswana pure economic loss in the form of viewers and advertising, which was the way the applicant generated revenue. The remedies sought by eBotswana were a declaratory and mandatory order which were granted, and the quantum of damages also sought was left for later adjudication by the court.

B. Passing Off

150. The essence of an action for passing off is to protect a business against misrepresentation of a particular kind, namely that the business, goods or services of the representor are that of the plaintiff or are associated therewith.[183] It protects against deception as to a trade source or a business connection.[184] There are three elements, which are sometimes called the 'classical trinity'. These elements are goodwill/reputation, misrepresentation and likelihood of damages or actual damages.[185]

151. Goodwill is described in the case law as the attractive force that brings in the customer. It is, in effect, the ability of a particular brand to persuade customers to purchase goods or services by identifying them as originating from a particular business. The attractive force can be anything from recognition of origination, satisfaction, safety, and much more. The circumstances of each case will be different, but often the necessary goodwill can be established by adducing evidence of sales figures, advertising spent for the products, press coverage, awards, web pages or social media references. If this material is not sufficient then survey or witness evidence as to the link made by consumers between the 'get up' of the products and the identity of the claimant will also be useful – albeit survey evidence is inherently difficult to adduce and always needs to be carefully considered before being commissioned.

183. *Caterham Car Sales & Coachworks Ltd v. Birkin Cars (Pty) Ltd* 1998 (3) SA 938 (SCA).
184. *F W Woolworth and Co (Zim) (Pvt) Ltd v. The Store and Another* 1998 (2) ZLR 402 (S).
185. *Unilever P.L.C and Another v. Vimco (Pvt) Ltd and Another* 2004 (2) ZLR 253 (H); *Zimbabwe Gelatine (Pvt) Ltd v. Cairns Food (Pvt) Ltd* SC-130-2002; *Zapchem Detergent Manufacturers CC v. Polaris Zimbabwe (Pvt) Ltd* 2003 (1) ZLR 481 (H); *Polaris Zimbabwe (Pvt) Ltd v. Zapchem Detergent Mfrs CC* 2004 (2) ZLR 351 (S).

152. A misrepresentation is an untrue or misleading statement of fact made by one party to another, the statement then inducing that other party into the contract. The test used in establishing misrepresentation for purposes of passing off is whether the statement by the defendant to the public leads the public or likely to lead the public to believe that the goods or services offered by him are the goods or services of the plaintiff. In order to prove passing off, the plaintiff has to demonstrate misrepresentation by the defendant to the public leading the public or likely to lead the public to believe that the goods or services offered by him are the goods or services of the plaintiff. The misrepresentation must create a false belief of connection that the two products are the same in the mind of the consumer. As such, it is a representation by one person that his business or merchandise is that of another or that it is associated with that of another. To determine whether a representation amounts to passing off, one enquires whether there is a reasonable likelihood that members of the public may be confused into believing that the business of one is connected with that of another. Misrepresentation can occur in a number of ways. It may relate to the product itself or to get-up, which is the product's packaging and presentation, the name used as well as imitation of symbols used to establish the plaintiff's reputation.

153. In order to succeed in the action of passing off, plaintiffs ought to demonstrate that they possess a reputation or goodwill that is associated with their goods or services and that there has been a misrepresentation by the defendant which has led to confusion and finally that misrepresentation has caused damage to the plaintiff's reputation or goodwill in the plaintiff's goods or services. Plaintiffs need not prove that actual damage to their goodwill has occurred unless they intend to seek remedies such as account of profits, which would mean the defendant would have had to have made a profit from the misrepresentation. It is enough for the plaintiff to establish the likelihood of damages. There is an existence of a likelihood of damages if they are reasonably foreseeable.

154. There are defences available for an action of passing off. Thus, in a suit for passing off, apart from denying the plaintiff's allegations generally, the defendant may be able to plead the following in defence in his case:

(a) The defendant may prove that the plaintiff's business is either fraudulent or forbidden by law. If any particular business could be shown to be a fraudulent business or one forbidden by law or one which the public policy of law was to prevent, then in those cases, the proprietor cannot claim protection from the court. For example, if a trader who sells through street markets counterfeit versions of sound recordings and DVDs bearing a famous trademark might not be allowed to rely on his sales to maintain a passing-off action against another counterfeiter who has come into the market after him.
(b) The field of activities of the parties is completely different. If the field of activity of the plaintiff and the defendant is different it gives a valid defence to the defence that since the goods and services are different no confusion and deception can take place among the consumers regarding respective trademarks.

(c) The mark complained of is not distinctive of the plaintiff's business and there is no likelihood of passing off by reason of the defendant's use of the mark. In *Gledhill v. British Perforated Toilet Paper*, the plaintiffs had for many years prior to 1902 sold rolls of paper under the name 'Gledhill's paper' and it was distinctive of the paper of the plaintiff. About 1902, the defendant commenced to manufacture and supply coils or papers for use in Gledhill's cash tills and in connection therewith, they used the word 'Gledhill' to distinguish them as they alleged from coils for other makes of tills. But subsequently, it was no longer distinctive of the goods of the plaintiff. Action to restrain the defendant from using the trademark 'Gledhill' was dismissed.

(d) The defendant may plead that the plaintiff has abandoned his mark and that the defendant has either already moved for rectification of register for removal of a mark or proposed to do so. Where a mark is abandoned, it may become common to trade. When abandoned, the mark may be appropriated by another person. The onus is on the defendant to prove abandonment.

(e) Where the plaintiff has given consent or encouraged the use of the mark.

(f) Where the plaintiff cannot demonstrate damage or loss he/she suffered.

(g) The defendant may successfully plead and establish that the alleged misrepresentation was made by his employee outside the scope of his authority and contrary to express instructions.

(h) The defendant's mark represents his own name which he has the right to use. 'A man is entitled to carry on his business in his own name so long as he does not do anything more than that to cause confusion with the business of another, and so long he does it honestly.'

(i) Delay on the part of the plaintiff after being aware of the use of the mark by the defendant is a defence in the hands of the defendant. Where non-user of a trademark is for a long period and that by reason it has lost its distinctiveness, the delay provides a good defence for refusing an injunction. Deliberate infringement or passing off is a continuing wrong, and therefore, interim relief will not be denied on the sole ground of delay especially when strong prima facie is made out.

155. The remedies available to a plaintiff in an action of passing off depending on the circumstances are an interdict, damages or an account of the defendant's profits, search and seizure and delivery up or destruction of the infringing articles.

C. *Injurious Falsehood*

156. The origins of injurious falsehood lie around the late sixteenth and the early seventeenth centuries in the action of slander of title to land. As such, it was not yet of any direct relevance as a tort of unfair competition. The earliest cases of 'injurious falsehood', which arose in the late sixteenth century, involved oral aspersions cast upon the plaintiff's ownership of land, because of which he was prevented from leasing or selling it. Hence slander of title, sometimes slander of goods, or disparagement of title, or disparagement of goods, or trade libel, or unfair competition, or interference with prospective advantage. This species of Aquilian liability is recognised in the sphere of unlawful competition as 'injurious falsehood'. It originated from the policy consideration that fair and honest competition is open to anyone, even if it involves interference with the trade of others, but that no one is permitted to carry on trade by fraudulent misstatement, either in respect of its own business or with reference to the business of its competitor.[186]

157. In order to prove a prima facie case of injurious falsehood, the plaintiff must prove that:[187]

(a) the defendant intentionally made false statements disparaging the plaintiff's property, goods or business interests;
(b) publication of the false statement to the third persons;
(c) malice by the defendant;
(d) proof of actual harm to the plaintiff's business or profession, caused by the malicious statement.

186. *Combrinck v. De Kock* (1887-1888) 5 SC 405 at 415; *Schultz v. Butt* 1986 (3) SA 667 (A).
187. *International Tobacco v. United Tobacco* 1955 (2) SA 1 (W).

Chapter 3. Private Regulation

158. While the public interest dictates that sports and commerce should be regulated publicly, it is also important to note that the main justification on which public regulation is pursued, ensuring that participants whose skill, effort, and talent lead to the generation of revenue are rewarded for this skill, effort, and talent, is rooted in the idea, often protected through private regulatory means, that intellectually property rights should be protected so as to encourage continuing ingenuity. And because the law recognises that there is no better placed, or motivated, party to protect these rights than the individual, the protection of these rights has been left to the individual as part of the private regulation framework. To this end, Zimbabwean sports law recognises that participants in sports should benefit from revenues generated as a result of the exploitation of the interest generated from their skill, effort, and talent for economic gain. It does so in two main ways.

159. First, the Constitution recognises that participants should benefit from revenues generated as a result of the exploitation of the interest generated from their skill, effort, and talent for economic gain. To this end, section 61(5) of the Constitution provides that every person has the right to freedom of expression, which but this does not include incitement to violence, advocacy of hatred or hate speech, and malicious injury to a person's reputation or dignity, or, malicious or unwarranted breach of a person's right to privacy. For instance, the use of a person's image, name or likeness in an advertisement without his or her consent will amount to defamation if it has the effect of reducing the reputation of the person in the eyes of right-thinking members of the public. This may, for example, arise where a person is linked to a product or service which is in some way derogatory in the circumstances, or where the creation of an impression that the person has been paid to endorse a particular product is defamatory. The appropriation of another's name or likeness is a recognisable ground for the invasion of privacy. This includes the use of a person's name or likeness in an advertisement without that person's consent. Separately, there is legislation that is in place to protect copyright and trademark. This legislation effectively gives effect to the Constitution and establishes the rights that fall to participants and circumstances in which these rights are violated are outlined and outlawed. Violations of the law typically occur when someone uses a person's image, name or likeness without their consent. Beyond this, the common law recognises that all natural and legal persons can market their brands and profit from doing so. Such marketing may take the form of the use of the person's name, image, photograph, likeness or voice in advertisements. Alternatively, the advertisement may refer to the celebrity's name or image and thus link it to the product. This has given rise to a crop of personality rights which, broadly speaking, are those rights that protect well-known personalities or celebrities from the unlawful use of their name, image, signature or persona. The right is negative in nature and comprises the individual's right to publicity and privacy. The individual's right to publicity gives him or her right to keep his or her image and likeness from unauthorised commercial exploitation, while the right of privacy grants the individual the right to keep his or her life out of public scrutiny regardless of the fact that he or she may be a national icon.

160. Second, the law empowers anyone whose personality rights have been violated to pursue the appropriate redress depending on the nature of the violation. For instance, if the violation is constitutional, then the courts can be approached. And, because personality rights are protected in terms of the Constitution, this can even be done in the public interest. If the violation is rooted in statute, then a party can always look for redress in the most appropriate way. The state obviously retains the right to treat the matter as a criminal, and thus public, issue. However, this does not preclude a party from mounting a civil action for redress. Where this is too complicated, or impossible, to do, there remains room for the offended party to bring an action rooted in the common law for redress. Such action can be based on such grounds as unjustified enrichment, or can be initiated in order to secure such remedies as interdict, restitution, or damages, depending on the circumstances.

Part V. COVID-19 and Its Impact on National Sport

§1. Introduction

161. Coronavirus 2019 (COVID-19) has wreaked havoc on the whole world since the Director General of the World Health Organization declared the outbreak of the disease as a Public Health Emergency of International Concern on 30 January 2020. In Zimbabwe, the first case of COVID-19 was recorded on 20 March 2020 and, in line with the approach adopted by several states, the state quickly declared a state of disaster on the same day.[188]From that time on, the number of cases of people returning positive tests for COVID-19 rose steadily. This prompted the government to unveil a ZWL 18 billion Economic Recovery and Stimulus Package aimed at revitalising the economy and providing relief to individuals, families, small businesses, and industries impacted by the economic slowdown caused by the COVID-19 pandemic. The main aim of the Package was to provide liquidity support to all the productive sectors of the economy and protect employment through the prevention and minimisation of COVID-19 effects.

§2. Legislative Measures and Their Impact on Sport

162. There have been no laws enacted for the sole purpose of governing sport during the pandemic. However, once the state decided that it would take measures to address the COVID-19 situation, the president declared a 'National Lockdown and Prohibition of Gatherings' for a twenty-one-day period commencing on 30 March 2020. This was accompanied by the enactment of the Public Health (COVID-19 Prevention, Containment and Treatment) Regulations.[189] These regulations, *inter alia*, carried restrictions on all manner of activities to ensure that the lockdown would take effect. For instance, there were provisions permitting the entry of citizens and residents to the country if they would be detained, isolated or quarantined in any place for a period of twenty-one days. There were also provisions which automatically extended permits of foreign nationals such that the lockdown period would not count towards their permitted period of stay in thc country.

188. Section 113 of the Constitution.
189. Statutory Instrument 77 of 2020.

163. The effect of compliance with the regulations was, effectively, to bring all sporting activity in the country to a halt.

164. Importantly for the present purpose, the regulations were also significant for athletes. Few athletes in Zimbabwe earn significant money from their participation in sports. In addition, a significant portion of the revenues generated in Zimbabwean sport is generated from 'gate takings.' Therefore, outlawing gatherings had a significant negative impact on athletes' wages and livelihoods. To limit the impact that the regulations had on the livelihoods of athletes in mid-2020, the Zimbabwean Government set up a COVID-19 relief fund. The fund was intended to help registered national sports associations, academies, athletes support personnel, individual athletes and community clubs stay afloat during the global health crisis. An equivalent of USD 2.7 million was committed to the fund and disbursements were made in an equitable manner. In football, which is particularly popular and which arguably relies on 'gate takings' the most among sports, the diminished earnings due to the lack of 'gate takings' also prompted the national football authority, ZIFA, to request a stimulus package from FIFA to help the sport survive.[190]

§3. Sports Measures to Restart Sport

165. Over time, and consistent with the practice in other states, COVID-19 regulations in Zimbabwe were frequently revisited to ensure that the country's response to the evolving COVID-19 situation always remained appropriate. Importantly for sport, this led to a progressive easing of restrictions headlined by the decision at the government level to allow social gatherings of up to fifty people.[191]

166. Once this occurred, stakeholders in sports, including the Ministry, the Sport and Recreation Council (SRC), the Olympic Committee, national sports federations, and clubs began to work to ensure that there was a gradual resumption of sporting activity in the country. This culminated in the SRC allowing the resumption of so-called low-risk sporting activities such as archery, cricket, chess, draft, table tennis, cycling, rolling, polo, shooting, tennis, horse racing, badminton, lawn bowls, triathlon, wood ball, motorsports, rowing, archery, angling, shooting, and swimming could resume.

167. At the same time, there was a constant assessment of what it would take to resume high-risk revenue-generating sports such as football. The challenge of this was that the cost of doing so was quite high. Using the example of football, Dandah

190. Gerald Dandah & Manase Kudzai Chiweshe (2021): Zimbabwe Premier Soccer League in the Context of COVID-19, Journal of Global Sport Management, DOI: 10.1080/24704067.2021.1899768.
191. XinhuaNet, 'Zimbabwe resumes low-risk sporting activities after easing of lockdown restrictions' available at:
http://www.xinhuanet.com/english/2021-03/04/c_139783885.htm#:~:text=Zimbabwe%20resumes%20low%2Drisk%20sporting%20activities%20after%20easing%20of%20lockdown%20restrictions,-Source%3A%20Xinhua%7C%202021&text=HARARE%2C%20March%204%20(Xinhua),by%20the%20government%20this%20week.

and Chiweshe computed that 'one of the key CAF recommendations for football to return on the menu was that each club's players and officials had to be tested using the recommended PCR tests. These could be obtained at a cost of US$65 per test kit. This meant that a team of 40 players and staff would demand US$2600 per week to comply with the safety requirements. For all the 18 teams in the Premier League, the budget world amount to US$46 800 per week'. This was a cost that most teams, already reliant on 'gate takings,' could not meet.[192]

168. In time, however, as the numbers of people contracting and dying from COVID-19 reduced, there was a shift in law which allowed for a return to sport. This was spearheaded by Statutory Instrument 81 of 2021 which provided that sportspersons engaged in medium or high risk sports may resume sporting activities with effect from the date of promulgation of the Public Health (COVID-19 Prevention, Containment and Treatment) (National Lockdown) (No. 2) (Amendment) Order, (No. 18). This effectively meant medium risk sports like Softball, Weightlifting, Power lifting, Gymnastics, Baseball, Darts, Dodgeball, Korfball, Pool, Sailing, Skateboarding, Gymnasiums, and high-risk sports like Football, Wrestling, Boxing, Basketball, Volleyball, Karate, Taekwondo, Netball, Handball, Judo, Hockey, Rugby, Bodybuilding, Squash, Wushu, Tug of War, and Kickboxing could resume.

169. Importantly though, there were conditions attached to resumption. Notably, PCR/Rapid-Antigen testing had to be done for all players, officials, and club staff at least 48 hours prior to commencement of training. Rapid-Antigen/ PCR tests also had to be done within every fourteen days of training from the last test. Testing also had to be done for all players, officials, and club staff at least 48 hours prior to the commencement of competition and friendly matches. Thereafter testing would be required after every fourteen days whichever was earlier. Similarly, there had to be testing 48 hours before games. All facilities (stadia) had to be disinfected before each game. There was the requirement that no spectators would be allowed. Further, all facilities such as showers and changing rooms had to be disinfected regularly and register kept. Sharing of sports equipment and apparel, towels, and other laundry; consumables and receptacles thereof, such as water bottles and cups; Personal Protective Equipment (PPE) in the form of face masks was prohibited. PPE in the form of face masks, tissues, wipe, and alcohol-based sanitiser also had to be available for distribution to athletes and members of the associated sports staff. All teams also had to keep a logbook of all athletes and associated sports staff entering and exiting the stadia and keep such logbooks for inspections by SRC enforcement officers at any time within thirty days from the date of the event to which it relates took place. In addition, no liquor or food could be served at stadia except water. The SRC also required detailed training schedules and venues to be submitted to its offices and they also demanded details of Club Compliance Officers to ensure full

192. Gerald Dandah & Manase Kudzai Chiweshe (2021): Zimbabwe Premier Soccer League in the Context of COVID-19, Journal of Global Sport Management, DOI: 10.1080/24704067.2021.1899768.

compliance with COVID-19 national and international protocols. The law also recommended the vaccination of athletes as per the National Vaccination Roll Out Programme.

170. At all times, however, the national leadership retained the authority to place a halt to sporting activities. For instance, following a new surge in new infections, on 12 June 2021, Vice President Constantino Chiwenga, also the Minister of Health and Child Care, announced that all public gatherings and sporting activities had been banned as part of new measures to contain the spread of COVID-19. This prompted the SRC to 'notify members of the public that pursuant to the statement by the Honourable Vice President of Zimbabwe … ALL sporting activities and events would be suspended with effect from Monday, 14th June 2021 until further notice. All national sports associations, clubs, gyms and related stakeholders were bound to abide by this suspension without exception'.[193]

§4. Conclusion

171. As the COVID-19 situation across the world continues to evolve, the same is true in Zimbabwe. Measures continue to be put in place to allow the safe transition back to sport. Barriers to participation in sporting activities have also been lifted as the number of vaccinated people has continued to rise. Presently, people can participate in any sporting activity as long as they respect and abide by prescribed Health and Safety Protocols. Going forward, sport is on course to pick up from where it was prior to COVID-19.

193. Sports Reporter, New Zimbabwe, 'Zimbabwe Suspends Sporting Activities Again Due To Covid-19' available at: https://www.newzimbabwe.com/zimbabwe-suspends-sporting-activities-again-due-to-covid-19/

Appendix I

CHAPTER 25:15

SPORTS AND RECREATION COMMISSION ACT

Act 15/1991, 22/2001 (s. 4)

1 Short title

This Act may be cited as the Sports and Recreation Commission Act [*Chapter 25:15*].

2 Interpretation

In this Act –
'Board' means the Sports and Recreation Board of Commissioners referred to in section *four*;
'club' means any group of persons associated together for the purposes of –

(a) sporting or recreational activities on a communal, district, regional, provincial, national or international basis; or
(b) participating in an organized league for sporting or recreational activities; or
(c) any sporting or recreational activities if members of the public are admitted to the club, whether by way of introduction or sponsorship or upon payment of a fee or subscription or otherwise;

'Commission' means the Sports and Recreation Commission established by section *three*;
'Director-General' means the Director-General of the Commission appointed in terms of section twenty-four;
'member' means the chairman or any other member of the Board referred to in subsection (1) of section five;
'Minister' means the Minister of Sports, Recreation and Culture or any other Minister to whom the President may, from time to time, assign the administration of this Act;
'national association' means any group or body of persons operating in Zimbabwe and having as its principal object the promotion or organization on a national basis of –

(a) any particular sport; or
(b) any recreational activity;
'recreation' includes any form of recreational activity which is not a sport;

'recreational facility' means –

(a) a playing field, open space, lake including an artificial lake, reservoir, river, pool or pond which is available for sports or recreation;
(b) a sports hall, pavilion or theatre; or
(c) a hall used for indoor sports or recreation or a court used for ball or other games;

and includes such facilities within factories and work places;
'register' means a register kept in terms of subsection (1) of section *twenty-nine*;
'sport' means any of the competitive sports and games set out in the First Schedule.

PART II: SPORTS AND RECREATION COMMISSION AND SPORTS AND RECREATION BOARD OF COMMISSIONERS

3 Establishment of Sports and Recreation Commission

There is hereby established a commission, to be known as the Sports and Recreation Commission which shall be a body corporate capable of suing and being sued in its corporate name and, subject to this Act, of performing all acts that bodies corporate may by law perform.

4 Establishment of Sports and Recreation Board of Commissioners

(1) There shall be a Sports and Recreation Board of Commissioners constituted in terms of section *five*.
(2) Subject to this Act, the operations of the Commission shall be controlled and managed by the Board, acting through the Director-General and other employees of the Commission.

5 Constitution of Board

(1) The Board shall consist of –
   (a) a chairman and not fewer than five and not more than nine other members appointed by the Minister after consultation with the President and subject to such directions as the President may give him; and
   (b) the Director-General, who shall be an *ex officio* member of the Board.
(2) Members referred to in paragraph (*a*) of subsection (1) shall be appointed for their ability and experience in sport or administration or both or for their suitability otherwise for appointment.
(3) The members of the Board shall elect a vice-chairman of the Board from among themselves, and the vice-chairman shall exercise the functions of the chairman during any period that the chairman is unable to exercise his functions.

(4) Subject to subsection (5), the Minister may appoint any person to the Board as an alternate to any member referred to in paragraph *(a)* of subsection (1) and such member –

(a) shall act as a member only when the member to whom he is alternate is for any reason unable to exercise his functions on the Board;

(b) when acting as a member shall exercise the functions of the member to whom he is alternate:

Provided that the alternates to the chairman and vice-chairman of the Board shall not exercise the functions of the chairman or vice-chairman, as the case may be.

Provided that the alternates to the chairman and vice-chairman of the Board shall not exercise the functions of the chairman or vice-chairman, as the case may be.

(5) In appointing a person as an alternate to a member in terms of subsection (4), the Minister shall be bound by the same requirements for appointment as are applicable, in terms of subsections (1) and (2), to the appointment of members.

6 Terms and conditions of office of members

(1) Subject to this Part, a member shall hold office for such period, not exceeding three years, as the Minister may fix on his appointment.

(2) Subject to section *fourteen*, a member shall hold office on such conditions as the Minister may fix in relation to members generally.

(3) A retiring member shall be eligible for re-appointment as a member.

7 Disqualifications for appointment as member

The Minister shall not appoint a person as a member and no person shall be qualified to hold office as a member who –

(a) is not a citizen of Zimbabwe or is not permanently resident in Zimbabwe; or

(b) has, or is married to a person who has, a financial interest in any business or is, or is married to a person who is, engaged in any activity connected with any business, if in the opinion of the Minister, such financial interest or activity is likely to interfere with the impartial discharge by that person of his duties as a member; or

(c) has, in terms of a law in force in any country –

(i) been adjudged or otherwise declared insolvent or bankrupt and has not been rehabilitated or discharged; or

(ii) made an assignment to, or arrangement or composition with, his creditors which has not been rescinded or set aside; or

(d) has, within the period of five years immediately preceding the date of his proposed appointment, been convicted of an offence in Zimbabwe and sentenced to a term of imprisonment imposed without the option of a fine and has not received a free pardon.

8 Vacation of office by member

A member shall vacate his office and his office shall become vacant –

(a) one month after the date upon which he gives notice in writing to the Minister of his intention to resign, or on the expiry of such other period of notice as he and the Minister may agree; or
(b) on the date he begins to serve a sentence of imprisonment imposed in Zimbabwe without the option of a fine; or
(c) if he becomes disqualified in terms of paragraph (*a*), (*b*) or (*c*) of section *seven* to hold office as a member; or
(d) if he is required in terms of section *nine* to vacate his office; or
(e) if he is absent without the permission of the Board from two consecutive meetings of the Board of which he was given not less than seven days' notice.

9 Minister may dismiss or suspend members

(1) The Minister may require a member to vacate his office if the Minister is satisfied that the member –
  (a) has been guilty of any conduct that renders him unsuitable as a member; or
  (b) has failed to comply with the conditions of his office fixed by the Minister in terms of subsection (2) of section *six*; or
  (c) is mentally or physically incapable of or incompetent in carrying out his functions as a member.
(2) The Minister may suspend a member against whom criminal proceedings have been instituted for an offence in respect of which a sentence of imprisonment without the option of a fine may be imposed, and while that member is so suspended he shall not carry out any functions as a member.

10 Filling of vacancies on Board

On the death of, or the vacation of office by, a member, the Minister shall, subject to section *five*, appoint a person to fill the vacancy.

11 Meetings and procedure of Board

(1) The Board shall hold its first meeting on such date and at such place as the Minister may fix and thereafter the Board shall meet for the dispatch of business and adjourn, close and otherwise regulate its meetings and procedure as

it thinks fit: Provided that a meeting of the Board shall be held not less than six times in each financial year of the Commission.

(2) The chairman of the Board –

(a) may at any time convene a special meeting of the Board; and

(b) shall, on the written request of the Minister or not fewer than two members, convene a special meeting of the Board, which meeting shall be convened for a date no later than thirty days after his receipt of such request.

(3) Written notice of any special meeting convened in terms of subsection (2) shall be sent to each member no later than forty-eight hours before the meeting and shall specify the business for which the meeting has been convened.

(4) No business shall be discussed at a special meeting convened in terms of subsection (2) other than –

(a) such business as may be determined by the chairman of the Board, where he has convened the meeting in terms of paragraph (*a*) of that subsection; or

(b) the business specified in the request for the meeting, where he has convened the meeting in terms of paragraph (*b*) of that subsection.

(5) If the chairman and the deputy chairman are both absent from a meeting of the Board, the members present may elect one of their number to preside at that meeting as chairman.

(6) Half the members of the Board shall form a quorum at any meeting of the Board.

(7) All acts, matters or things authorised or required to be done by the Board may be decided by a majority vote at a meeting of the Board at which a quorum is present.

(8) Subject to section *fifteen*, at all meetings of the Board each member present shall have one vote on each question before the Board and, in the event of an equality of votes, the chairman shall have a casting vote in addition to a deliberative vote.

(9) Any proposal circulated among all members and agreed to in writing by a majority of all members shall have the same effect as a resolution passed at a duly constituted meeting of the Board and shall be incorporated in the minutes of the next succeeding meeting of the Board:

Provided that, if a member requires that such proposal be placed before a meeting of the Board, this subsection shall not apply to such proposal.

12 Committees of Board

(1) The Board may appoint such committees as it thinks necessary for the better exercise of its functions and shall vest in the committees such of its functions as are appropriate: Provided that the vesting of any functions in a committee shall not divest the Board of those functions in relation to any matter that has not been decided by the committee.

(2) Where it has established a committee in terms of subsection (1), the Board –

(a) shall appoint at least one member of the Board to be a member of the committee and shall designate that member, or one of those members, as the case may be, to be chairman of the committee; and
(b) subject to subsection (3), may appoint persons who are not members of the Board to be members of the committee.

(3) The Board shall not appoint a person to be a member of a committee if he is disqualified in terms of section *seven* from appointment as a member of the Board.

(4) The office of a member of a committee of the Board shall terminate –
(a) in the case of a member who is a member of the Board, upon his ceasing to be a member of the Board;
(b) in the case of a member who is not a member of the Board, if he would be required in terms of section *eight* to vacate his office had that section and paragraphs (*a*), (*b*) and (*c*) of section *seven* applied to him.

(5) Subject to this section and section *fourteen*, members of committees of the Board shall hold office on such conditions as the Board may fix for members of committees generally.

(6) The chairman of the Board may at any time and place convene a meeting of a committee of the Board.

(7) Subject to subsection (6) and sections *fifteen* and *eighteen*, the procedure to be followed at any meeting of a committee of the Board and the quorum at such a meeting shall be fixed by the Board.

(8) No decision or act of a committee of the Board or act done under the authority of a committee of the Board shall be invalid solely on the ground that –
(a) the committee consisted of fewer than the number of members, if any, fixed by the Board as constituting the membership of the committee; or
(b) a disqualified person acted as a member of the committee; at the time the decision was taken or the act was done or authorised if the duly appointed members of the committee who were present constituted a quorum.

13 Olympic Committee

(1) The Board shall ensure the election of an Olympic Committee in accordance with the Olympic Charter for the purpose of ensuring Zimbabwe's effective representation at each Olympic Games and for carrying out functions relating thereto.

(2) Members of the Olympic Committee shall hold office under such conditions as provided by the Olympic Charter and as approved by the Board.

14 Remuneration and expenses of members of Board and members of committees

Members of the Board and of committees of the Board shall be paid from the funds of the Commission –

(a) such remuneration, if any, as the Minister, with the approval of the Minister responsible for finance, may from time to time fix for such members generally; and
(b) such allowances, if any, as the Minister, with the approval of the Minister responsible for finance, may from time to time fix to meet any reasonable expenses incurred by such members in connection with the business of the Board or of the committees concerned, as the case may be.

15 Disclosure of interest of members of Board and members of committees

(1) If a member of the Board or of a committee of the Board or a spouse of such a member –
   (a) tenders for or acquires or holds a direct or indirect pecuniary interest in a contract with the Commission; or
   (b) knowingly acquires or holds a direct or indirect pecuniary interest in a company or association of persons applying or negotiating for a contract with the Commission; or
   (c) owns immovable property or a right in immovable property or a direct or indirect pecuniary interest in a company or association of persons which results in his private interests coming or appearing to come into conflict with his duties as a member;

   the member shall forthwith disclose the fact to the Board or to the committee, as the case may be.
(2) A member referred to in subsection (1) shall take no part in consideration or discussion of, or vote on, any question before the Board or the committee, as the case may be, which relates to any contract, right, immovable property or interest referred to in that subsection.
(3) The Director-General shall take no part in the consideration or discussion of any question before the Board which relates to the terms and conditions of his appointment as Director-General.

16 Validity of decisions and acts of Board

No decision or act of the Board or act done under the authority of the Board shall be invalid solely on the ground that –

(a) the Board consisted of fewer than the minimum number of persons for which provision is made in subsection (1) of section *five*;
(b) a disqualified person acted as a member; at the time the decision was taken or the act was done or authorized if the duly appointed members of the committee who were present constituted a quorum.

17 Execution of contracts and instruments by Commission

An agreement, contract or instrument approved by the Board may be entered into or executed on behalf of the Commission by any person or persons generally or specially authorized by the Board for that purpose.

18 Minutes of proceedings of Board and committees

(1) The Board shall cause minutes of all proceedings of and decisions taken at every meeting of the Board or of a committee of the Board to be entered in books kept for the purpose.
(2) Any minutes referred to in subsection (1) which purport to be signed by the chairman of the meeting to which the minutes relate or by the chairman of the next following meeting of the Board or the committee concerned, as the case may be, shall be accepted for all purposes as *prima facie* evidence of the proceedings of and decisions taken at the meeting concerned.

PART III: OBJECTS AND FUNCTIONS OF COMMISSION

19 Objects of the Commission

The objects of the Commission shall be –

(a) to co-ordinate, control, develop and foster the activities of sport and recreation;
(b) to ensure the proper administration of organisations undertaking the promotion of sport and recreation;
(c) to promote the highest standards of sportsmanship;
(d) to authorize national and international sporting and recreational activities;
(e) to advise the Government of the needs of sport and recreation;
(f) to endeavour to ensure that opportunities for sport and recreation are made available to all persons throughout Zimbabwe;
(g) to endeavour to provide coaches, instructors and courses for sports, either free or on the payment of reasonable fees;
(h) to assist registered national associations, registered clubs and schools in the recruitment of coaches and instructors;
(i) to endeavour to ensure that recreational facilities are established in such work places as the Board considers appropriate;
(j) to establish, maintain and operate establishments for the accommodation of visiting sports teams or recreational clubs, or groups of persons engaged in furtherance of the purposes of this Act;
(k) to undertake special projects, with the approval of the Minister, including fund raising, marketing and trading activities, in furtherance of the purposes of this Act;
(l) to negotiate with registered clubs and registered national associations to ensure that recreational facilities are fully utilised;
(m) to oversee training programmes for sportspersons;
(n) to develop, supervise and manage sporting facilities;

(o) to encourage the production of sporting goods;
(p) to determine, grant and supervise national sports awards to outstanding sportspersons and sports administrators.

20 Responsibilities of Commission to registered national associations

The Commission shall have the following responsibilities in relation to registered national associations –

(a) to ensure that membership of every such association is open to all clubs and schools *bona fide* engaging in the activity for which the association is responsible and being prepared to pay its dues and abide by its rules;
(b) to approve the annual estimates of such associations and to receive their audited annual accounts;
(c) to generally advise, assist and supervise such associations.

21 Powers of Commission

(1) Subject to this Act, for the carrying out of its objects the Commission shall have power to do or cause to be done, either by itself or through its agents, all or any of the things specified in the Second Schedule, either absolutely or conditionally and either solely or jointly with others.

22 Reports of the Board

(1) In addition to any report which the Board is required to submit to the Minister in terms of this Act or the Audit and Exchequer Act [*Chapter 22:03*], the Board –
    (a) shall submit to the Minister such other reports as the Minister may require;
    (b) may submit to the Minister such other reports as the Board may consider advisable;
    in regard to the operations, undertakings and property of the Commission.
(2) The Board shall give the Minister all such information relating to the undertakings of the Commission as the Minister may at any time require.
(3) The Minister may lay before Parliament a report submitted to him by the Board in terms of subsection (1).

23 Minister may give directions to Commission

(1) Subject to subsection (2), the Minister may give the Commission such written directions of a general character relating to the exercise of the Commission's functions as appear to the Minister to be requisite in the national interest.

(2) Before giving the Commission a direction in terms of subsection (1), the Minister shall inform the Board, in writing, of the proposed direction and the Board shall submit in writing to the Minister, within thirty days or such further period as the Minister may allow, its views on the proposal and its possible effects on the finances and other resources of the Commission.
(3) The Commission shall, with all due expedition, comply with any direction given to it in terms of subsection (1).
(4) Where the Commission has been given a direction in terms of subsection (1), the Board shall ensure that the direction and any views it has expressed thereon in terms of subsection (2) are set out in its annual report submitted in terms of the Audit and Exchequer Act [*Chapter 22:03*].

24 Director-General

(1) The Board shall appoint, subject to this Act and on such terms and conditions as the Board, with the approval of the Minister, may fix, a person approved by the Minister to be the Director-General.
(2) No person shall be appointed as Director-General and no person shall hold office as Director-General if he is not ordinarily resident in Zimbabwe.
(3) The Board shall terminate the appointment of the Director-General if he would be required in terms of paragraph (*b*), (*c*) or (*e*) of section *eight* to vacate his office had that section and paragraphs (*a*), (*b*) and (*c*) of section *seven* applied to him.
(4) Subject to the general control of the Board, the Director-General shall be responsible for –
   (a) managing the operations, undertakings and property of the Commission; and
   (b) giving effect to the decisions of the Board; and
   (c) supervising and controlling the activities of the employees of the Commission in the course of their employment.
(5) The Board may assign to the Director-General such of the functions of the Board as the Board thinks fit.
(6) Any assignment of functions in terms of subsection (5) may be made either generally or specially and subject to such reservations, restrictions and exceptions as the Board may determine, and may be revoked by the Board at any time.

PART IV: FINANCIAL PROVISIONS

25 Funds of the Commission

(1) The funds of the Commission shall consist of –
   (a) moneys appropriated for the purpose by Act of Parliament; and
   (b) levies raised in terms of section *twenty-six*; and

(c) loans which have been raised with the approval of the Minister responsible for finance; and
(d) entry fees to and miscellaneous takings at sporting and recreational events organized and administered by the Commission; and
(e) receipts from any trading or marketing activity carried on by the Commission itself or jointly with some other person or organization; and
(f) any other moneys to which the Commission may become entitled, whether through its activities in carrying out its objects or otherwise.

(2) The Commission shall invest its funds in a manner approved by the Minister and the Minister responsible for finance.

(3) The funds of the Commission shall, subject to the directions of the Minister, be chargeable with –
(a) the establishment and maintenance of schemes, projects or undertakings by the Commission for the development of any sport or recreation;
(b) the provision, development, maintenance and operation of recreational facilities;
(c) visits and tours, whether inside or outside Zimbabwe, by sportspersons and representatives of any sporting or recreational association or institution, whether Zimbabwean or otherwise;
(d) the holding of congresses or other functions for or in aid of any sport or recreation;
(e) the wages, salaries, fees or remuneration of persons employed by or acting for or on behalf of the Commission;
(f) the costs involved in acquiring accommodation for the use of the Commission;
(g) the administrative costs involved in the functioning of the Commission;
(h) any other costs, charges or expenses incurred by the Commission in the exercise of its functions in terms of this Act.

26 Levies

(1) Subject to such terms and conditions as may be prescribed, the Commission may impose a levy on –
(a) all registered national associations; and
(b) tickets sold for admission to any recreational facility in order to witness any sporting activity:

Provided that –
(i) any levy on registered national associations shall be imposed on all such associations without distinction unless the Minister in any particular case, on the application of the Commission, grants an exemption;
(ii) any levy on tickets sold shall not be more than ten *per centum* of the price of admission paid for the ticket.

(2) A levy imposed in terms of subsection (1) shall be calculated, paid and collected in such manner as may be prescribed.

27 Holding of funds by Commission

All moneys received by the Commission shall be paid into a banking account and no money shall be withdrawn therefrom except by means of a cheque or other instrument signed by such person or persons as may be authorized thereto by the Board.

28 Accounts and audit

(1) The Commission shall keep proper books of account.
(2) The Board shall appoint an auditor, who may be the Comptroller and Auditor-General or a person who is registered as a public auditor in terms of the Public Accountants and Auditors Act [*Chapter 27:12*].
(3) The Board shall prepare and submit to the Minister a statement of accounts in respect of each financial year of the Commission or such other period as the Minister may direct.
(4) The auditor shall examine the accounts of the Commission and make a report to the Board and to the Minister of the statement of accounts prepared in terms of subsection (3), and such report shall state whether or not in his opinion the statement of accounts gives a true and fair view of the state of the financial affairs of the Commission.
(5) In addition to the report referred to in subsection (4), the Minister may require the Board to obtain from its auditor such other report or statement in connection with the operations, undertakings and property of the Commission as the Minister may consider expedient.
(6) Without derogation from subsection (6) of section 9 of the Audit and Exchequer Act [*Chapter 22:03*], an auditor shall be entitled at all reasonable times to require to be produced to him all accounts and other records relating thereto kept by the Commission or its agents and to require from any member of the Board or any person employed by the Commission or its agents such information and explanations as in his opinion are necessary for the purposes of his audit.
(7) The Commission shall pay all of its expenses of carrying out the provisions of this section.

PART V: REGISTERED NATIONAL ASSOCIATIONS

29 Registration of national associations

(1) For the purposes of this Part the Commission shall keep and maintain a register of national associations.
(2) The register shall be open to inspection by any person at all reasonable times, free of charge, at the offices of the Commission.
(3) Every national association shall, within three months of the 1st September, 1991, or within thirty days of its coming into existence, whichever is the later, apply to the Commission for registration in the form and manner prescribed.

(4) As soon as is practicable after receiving an application in terms of subsection (3), the Board shall consider the application and, if it is satisfied –
(a) as to the suitability of the constitution and rules of the national association; and
(b) as to the good faith of the officers and members of the national association; and
(c) that the affairs of the national association will be properly managed;
the Board shall direct the Director-General to cause the national association and its constitution and rules to be registered.

(5) Where any amendment is made to the constitution or rules of a registered national association, or any alteration occurs in any of the matters or things in respect whereof particulars are required to be given as prescribed, such association shall forthwith give particulars in writing of such amendment or alteration, as the case may be, to the Commission.

(6) Upon receiving particulars of any amendment to the constitution or rules of a registered national association in terms of subsection (5), the Board shall, if it is satisfied as to the suitability of the amendment, direct the Director-General to cause the amendment to be registered.

(7) No provision of the constitution or rules of a registered national association, and no amendment thereof, shall be of any effect unless the constitution or rules or the amendment, as the case may be, is registered in terms of subsection (4) or (6).

(8) Every registered national association shall as soon as practicable after the end of its financial year submit to the Commission –
(a) a report on its activities during the previous year; and
(b) an audited balance sheet and income and expenditure account for that year.

(9) Every registered national association shall, as early as convenient before the commencement of its financial year, submit to the Commission its estimates of income and expenditure for the coming year and shall likewise submit any amendments to such estimates.

(10) If the Director-General considers that any estimates submitted in terms of subsection (9) are not in the best interests of the members of the association which submitted the report, he may, after discussing the estimates with the governing body of the association, make a report on the estimates to the Board.

(11) When a report is made to the Board in terms of subsection (10) the Board may, after hearing a duly authorized representative or representatives of the association concerned, require the association to amend its estimates.

30 Discipline of registered national associations

(1) Where the Board considers that any registered national association –
(a) has ceased to operate as a national association; or
(b) has failed to comply with any provision of this Act; or

(c) has conducted itself in a manner which is contrary to the national interest; the Board may, after affording the association concerned an opportunity of making representations in the matter, do either or both of the following –
   (i) suspend all or any of its officers;
   (ii) direct the Director-General to strike the association from the register.

(2) Where the Board has taken any action referred to in subparagraph (i) or (ii) of subsection (1) the Minister may on the recommendation of, or after consultation with, the Board appoint a committee to administer the affairs of the association concerned.

(3) A committee appointed in terms of subsection (2) shall have all the rights, duties and responsibilities of the governing body it has displaced but shall be answerable to the Board and not to the members of the national association.

(4) Where a committee has been appointed in terms of subsection (2) –
   (a) the name of the national association concerned shall, if it has been struck off the register, be restored to the register;
   (b) the committee shall, as soon as practicable, take step for the appointment of a new governing body of the association concerned in accordance with the constitution and rules of the association.

PART VI: GENERAL

31 National Colours

(1) The President shall, by statutory instrument, declare the National Colours of Zimbabwe.

(2) The Commission may award National Colours to any individual, team or association and by statutory instrument make rules governing such awards.

(3) No person shall wear or display the National Colours otherwise than in accordance with an award by the Commission in terms of subsection (2) or in accordance with an award made before the 1st September, 1991, under the Zimbabwe Youth Council Act [*Chapter 25:19*] which shall be deemed to be an award made by the Commission.

(4) Any person who contravenes subsection (3) shall be guilty of an offence and shall be liable to a fine not exceeding level three. [Subsection as amended by section 4 of Act No. 22 of 2001]

32 Appeals to Administrative Court

(1) Any person who is aggrieved by a decision of the Board or the Commission in terms of this Act may appeal against the decision to the Administrative Court.

(2) An appeal in terms of this section shall be lodged with the Registrar of the Administrative Court within twenty-one days of the date of the decision appealed against.

(3) The Administrative Court Act [*Chapter 7:01*] shall apply in relation to the composition, procedure and powers of the Administrative Court on an appeal in terms of this section.

33 Protection of employment of members of national teams

Where any person has been selected to represent Zimbabwe in any sport or recreational event such person shall not suffer any reduction in seniority, leave, salary or other benefits or be discharged from his employment solely on the ground that he is required to be away from his place of employment for the purposes of such representation.

34 Exemption of Commission from liability

No liability shall attach to the Commission or to any employee or agent of the Commission or to the Board or to a member of the Board or any committee of the Board for any loss or damage sustained by any person as a result of the *bona fide* exercise by an employee or agent of the Commission or by the Board or by a member of the Board or any committee of the Board of any function or power conferred upon the Commission by this Act: Provided that this section shall not be construed so as to prevent any person from recovering by action in any competent court compensation for any loss or damage sustained by him which was caused by negligence.

35 Amendment of First Schedule

The Minister may from time to time, after consultation with the Commission, by statutory instrument, amend the First Schedule by the addition thereto or the deletion therefrom of any sport or game.

36 Regulations

(1) The Minister may, after consultation with the Commission, make regulations providing for all matters which by this Act are required or permitted to be prescribed or which, in his opinion, are necessary or convenient to be provided for in order to carry out or give effect to this Act.
(2) Regulations made in terms of subsection (1) may provide for –
  (a) the amount, payment and collection of levies imposed in terms of section *twenty-six*;
  (b) the form and manner in which applications for registration shall be made and dealt with;
  (c) the formation, registration and functions of provincial, regional or district sporting or recreational associations, and the circumstances in which their registration may be cancelled;
  (d) the formation, registration and functions of clubs and the circumstances in which their registration may be cancelled;
  (e) the membership of registered clubs, and the fees and subscriptions payable for such membership or for the use of their facilities;

(f) accounts and other records to be kept by registered national associations and registered clubs;
(g) the registration of recreational facilities, the cancellation of such registration, and rights of access to registered recreational facilities;
(h) prohibiting –
    (i) unregistered associations and clubs and members thereof from competing or dealing with registered associations and clubs and members thereof and vice-versa;
    (ii) persons who are not members of registered clubs from being eligible for an award of National Colours;
(i) the conduct and administration of national and international sporting or recreational activities;
(j) the carrying on by the Commission or by any registered national association or registered club of trading or commercial activities.

37 Savings

On and after the 1st September, 1991 –

(a) all the assets and liabilities which immediately before the 1st September, 1991, were assets and liabilities of the Zimbabwe Sports and Recreation Council shall pass by succession to the Sports and Recreation Commission, which shall have all the powers, duties and obligations in relation to such assets and liabilities as are conferred by this Act in relation to its assets and liabilities;
(b) all bonds, hypothecations, title deeds, documents, charges, agreements, contracts, notes, instruments and working arrangements subsisting immediately before the 1st September, 1991, shall be of full force and effect against or in favour of the Sports and Recreation Commission and enforceable as fully and effectively as if, instead of the Zimbabwe Sports and Recreation Council, the Sports and Recreation Commission had been named therein and had been a party thereto;
(c) it shall not be necessary for the Registrar of Deeds to make any endorsement on the title deeds or in his registers in respect of any immovable property or any rights or obligations under a mortgage, hypothecation, pledge, bond, note or charge vested in or imposed upon the Sports and Recreation Commission under this section, but the Registrar of Deeds shall, when so requested in writing by the Board in relation to any particular such immovable property, mortgage, hypothecation, pledge, bond, note or charge, cause, free of charge, the name of the Sports and Recreation Commission to be substituted for that of the Zimbabwe Sports and Recreation Council on the appropriate title deed or other document in the appropriate register.

Selected Bibliography

Books and Articles

Agencies. *What the Sports Betting Levy Means for Zimbabwe Sports*, https://bulawayo24.com/index-id-sports-sc-local-byo-139456.html (accessed 20 March 2020).

BBC Sport. *ICC Suspends Zimbabwe Cricket for Political Interference*, https://www.bbc.com/sport/cricket/49038834 (accessed 20 July 2019).

Peter Cane & Joanne Conaghan. *The New Oxford Companion to Law.* OUP 2008, https://www.oxfordreference.com/view/10.1093/acref/9780199290543.001.0001/acref-9780199290543-e-1445 (accessed 12 June 2020).

Kevin Carpenter. *Match-Fixing-The Biggest Threat to Sport in the 21st Century?*, http://www.responsiblegambling.eu/wp-content/uploads/2016/06/Match-Fixing%E2%80%94The-Biggest-Threat-to-Sport-in-the-21st-Century.pdf (accessed 12 June 2020).

Gerald Dandah & Manase Kudzai Chiweshe (2021): Zimbabwe Premier Soccer League in the Context of COVID 19, Journal of Global Sport Management, DOI: 10.1080/24704067.2021.1899768

Chronicle Sport. *Muchechetere on Good Governance*, https://www.chronicle.co.zw/muchechetere-on-good-governance/ (accessed 18 November 2019).

European Commission. *European Commission's White Paper on Sport,* 11 July 2007, COM (2007) 391, https://eur-lex.europa.eu/legal-content/EN/TXT/?uri=CELEX%3A52007DC0391 (accessed 20 March 2020).

Geoffrey Feltoe. *A Guide to Administrative Law and Local Government Law in Zimbabwe*. Legal Resources Foundation, Harare 2012.

Geoffrey Feltoe. *A Guide to the Zimbabwean Law of Delict.* Legal Resources Foundation, Harare, 2013.

Footballers Union of Zimbabwe. *Anti-doping*, http://www.fuz.co.zw/playerservices.php?id=8 (accessed 20 March 2020).

Nancy Gillen. *Zimbabwe Olympic Committee Run Governance Strategy Workshops for National Sport Associations*, https://www.insidethegames.biz/articles/1084524/zimbabwe-olympic-committee-governance (accessed 20 March 2020).

Edward Grayson. *Sport and the Law*. 2nd ed., Butterworths, London 1994.

Munyaradzi Gwisai. *Labour and Employment Law in Zimbabwe: Relations of Work under Neo-Colonial Capitalism.* Zimbabwe Labour Centre, Harare, 2006.

ICC. *25 Years of Zimbabwe in Test Cricket*, https://www.icc-cricket.com/news/498590 (accessed 30 July 2019).

Selected Bibliography

Mark James & Fiona Deeley. 'The Standard of Care in Sports Negligence Cases'. *Entertainment and Sports Law Journal* 1, no. 1 (2002): 104–108.

Tapiwa G. Kasuso, *Labour Law Zimbabwe Open University Labour Law Module*. ZOU, Harare, 2019.

Tapiwa G. Kasuso. 'Resignation of an Employee under Zimbabwean Labour Law'. *Midlands State University Law Review* 4 (2017): 3.

Petros Kausiyo. *Sadomba Hits Back*, https://www.herald.co.zw/sadomba-hits-back/ (accessed 14 January 2020).

Alistair J. Kerr. *Principles of the Law of Contract*. 4th ed., Butterworths, London, 1989.

Eddie T.C. Lam. 'The Roles of Governance in Sport Organizations'. *Journal of Power, Politics and Governance* 2 (2014): 19.

Law in Sport. *INTERPOL Integrity in Sport Bi-Weekly Bulletin – 30 July 2019 – 12 August 2019*, https://www.lawinsport.com/topics/item/interpol-integrity-in-sport-bi-weekly-bulletin-30-july-2019-12-august-2019 (accessed 1 August 2019).

Max Loubser, et al. *The Law of Delict in South Africa* 4, 3rd ed., Oxford University Press, Oxford 2018.

Lovemore Madhuku. *Labour Law in Zimbabwe*. Weaver Press, Harare, 2015.

Esau Mandipa. *A Critical Analysis of the Legal and Institutional Frameworks for the Realisation of the Rights of Persons with Disabilities in Zimbabwe*. University of Pretoria, South Africa Unpublished Master's Thesis 2011.

Tony Meenaghan. 'The Role of Sponsorship in the Marketing Communications Mix'. *The International Journal of Advertising* 10 (1991).

Matthew J. Mitten, et al. *Sports Law and Regulation: Cases, Materials and Problems*. Walters Kluwer Law and Business, Aspen, 2009.

Sikhumbuzo Moyo. *Doping Claims Rock Zimbabwe Athletics*, https://www.chronicle.co.zw/doping-claims-rock-zimbabwe-athletics/ (accessed 18 November 2019).

Bernard James Mullin, Stephen Hardy & William Anthony Sutton. *Sport Marketing*. Human Kinetics, Illinois, 1993, 254.

Newsday. *PSL to Sniff for Drugs*, https://www.newsday.co.zw/2019/03/psl-to-sniff-for-drugs/ (accessed 20 March 2020).

Jimcall Pfumorodze & Emma Chitsove. *The Law in Zimbabwe*, https://www.nyulawglobal.org/globalex/Zimbabwe1.html (accessed 23 March 2020).

PSL. *Premier Soccer League Rules and Regulations*, Order 3.5., http://www.fuz.co.zw/statutes/0-1522155406PSL%20Rules%20and%20Regulations%20Final.pdf (accessed 2 March 2020).

Dennis M. Sandler & David Shani. 'Sponsorship and the Olympic Games: The Consumer Perspective'. *Sport Marketing Quarterly* 2 (1993): 38.

Frank I. Schechter. 'The Rational Basis of Trade Mark Protection'. *Harvard Law Review* 40 (1927): 813.

South African Institute for Drug – Free Sport. *Anti-doping Rules 2019*, https://www.drugfreesport.org.za/wp-content/uploads/2019/04/SAIDS-Anti-Doping-Rules-2019.pdf (accessed 20 March 2020).

Sports Reporter, New Zimbabwe, 'Zimbabwe Suspends Sporting Activities Again Due To Covid-19'available at: https://www.newzimbabwe.com/zimbabwe-suspends-sporting-activities-again-due-to-covid-19/

Staff Reporter. '*Dynamos Lose Against Guthrie Zhokinyi*.' 10 February 2017, https://bulawayo24.com/index-id-sports-sc-soccer-byo-104180.html (accessed 12 June 2020).

Michael Jhon Tamayo. *What Is Governance?*, https://tamayaosbc.wordpress.com/2014/08/21/what-is-governance/ (accessed 25 March 2020).

Lesa Ukman. *IEG's Complete Guide to Sponsorship*. IEG, Chicago, 2004, 154.

World Olympians Association. *Zimbabwe Olympians Unite to Tackle Doping in Sport*, https://olympians.org/news/481/zimbabwe-olympians-unite-to-tackle-doping-in-sport/ (accessed 20 March 2020).

XinhuaNet, 'Zimbabwe resumes low-risk sporting activities after easing of lock-down restrictions' available at: http://www.xinhuanet.com/english/2021-03/04/c_139783885.htm#:~:text=Zimbabwe%20resumes%20low%2Drisk%20sporting%20activities%20after%20easing%20of%20lockdown%20restrictions,-Source%3A%20Xinhua%7C%202021&text=HARARE%2C%20March%204%20(Xinhua),by%20the%20government%20this%20week.

UNESCO. *What Is Doping?*, http://www.unesco.org/new/en/social-and-human-sciences/themes/anti-doping/youth-space/what-is-doping/ (accessed 30 November 2019).

Zimbabwe Government. *Introduction to Committees in Parliament*, https://www.parlzim.gov.zw/about-parliament/committee-system (accessed 23 May 2019).

ZOC. *Anti-doping in Sport Takes Centre Stage*, http://zoc.co.zw/anti-doping-in-sport-takes-centre-stage/ (accessed 20 March 2020).

Selected Bibliography

Table of Cases

Table of Legislation

National Legislation

Subsidiary Legislation

Table of Legislation

Index

The numbers here refer to paragraph numbers.

Index

www.ingramcontent.com/pod-product-compliance
Ingram Content Group UK Ltd.
Pitfield, Milton Keynes, MK11 3LW, UK
UKHW021239300926
15471UKWH00013B/762

9 789403 507668